UNITE THE STATES!

How America Can Become a Better Country in the 21st Century and Beyond

By Bob McClure V

Original written by
Robert McClure V

Mister Five Publications

Unite the States!

Written by Robert McClure V

First printing: 2012
Second printing: 2013
Third printing: 2017
Fourth printing: 2018

For additional information contact:
Bob McClure V
Bobmcclure55@gmail.com

PREFACE

One thing becoming more obvious every day to more people everywhere is that America is getting to be very hard to govern. Many cherished aspects of American life seem to be visible only in the rear-view mirror of History. Complaints are heard everywhere about how things just don't feel as good as they used to "back in the good old days". A majority of our citizens have convinced themselves that the things about America that they loved the most are all behind us, carried away in a strong current of events out of their control – out of anyone's control.

People wanting a different direction have little choice except to support politicians who promise change but deliver little more than slogans or expressions of sympathy. The resulting frustration is compounded by a bewildering complexity that has steadily grown in modern societies around the world. There seems to be no really safe haven and the distress is leading to fear, anger, and despair in many quarters.

Individuals appear suddenly on the public scene who present themselves as having the true vision upon which the country was founded. Many of them maintain that theirs is the only true message – that this country and its direction are theirs to define and administer. But in reality, the old Biblical advice to "beware of false prophets" is most true when politics and governments are involved.

This book is submitted for consideration as a stimulus for new discussions on how America can move forward, not back, to better achieve its original aims – in the twenty-first century and beyond.

FORWARD

In the decades before the American Revolution, philosophers of the Enlightenment generally held the concept of Democracy in low esteem. Monarchies ruled the nations and empires of the world and most political thought of the day regarded "the masses" as being incapable of the will to sustain any lasting government.

The crucial difference made by our founding fathers was to adopt something unique from the example of the Native Americans they met here: personal liberty and freedom. While not always traveling far from their roots, the natives seemed fleet of foot and free as individuals and often whole tribes moved through the forests, over the mountains, and across the prairies. It was a feature of life in the American colonies that was truly uplifting – even to those who would have had a life of privilege in their old country in Europe.

These concepts were alien to the cultures of the Old World, where people were born into rigidly-structured societies in which their "class" defined the course of their lives. The peasantries of Europe and Asia were culturally – and sometimes forcefully – bound to the same local areas where they were born. For many, the only way to break that bleak pattern was to sail westward across the Atlantic to the wild shores of America. Most of the European settlers coming here did so with the expectation of a rumored individual liberty. They deeply cherished it once finding they possessed it – and soon, a desire to keep it possessed them.

So, resident by resident, the culture changed in a profound, yet unannounced way. European-Americans knew they were innately different from the ancestors they left behind – so far away on the eastern side of the wide ocean. Now they were more alike than different, no matter who their parents might have been or where they might have lived.

Generally, Europeans didn't recognize this until after the Americans declared they had an inalienable right to be independent and "free" – whatever that meant. Having pulled a large chunk of the New World away from the proprietary claims of the other colonial powers just a few years earlier in a mutual war against France, the English king was outraged at the betrayal of trust. From his point of view the colonists had depended on England's support for a century and a half and had prospered more than any other society on earth – even his own. So there was a war – seven years long officially, starting off with five years of heated fighting.

In those days, the English army and navy were nearly pre-eminent in the world. They had beaten back the Spanish ascendency in Europe two centuries earlier and were still battling them, the French, and the Dutch around the globe in the European rush to carve up the entire world into colonies that were to be economically and politically exploited. The rag-tag army assembled by the American colonists was laughable by the standards of the day, but they wouldn't be defeated – on their home soil. In England's global strategy of colonization, the defeat in America was an annoyance rather than any strategic blow. George Washington and his cohorts were never going to challenge England's interests in India or Africa. The issue of revenge for the affront would wait for another generation to settle.

The troubling concept for thoughtful Europeans of the day was the "freedom" and "liberty" that Americans so loudly espoused. Those were dangerous ideas indeed for societies that depended upon the subjugation of their own peasantries and ruthless suppression of native peoples in their colonies. America now has one of the oldest functioning governments in the world – a mark of true political success. From the time of this country's inception we have justifiably felt blessed. History has demonstrated that it was the marriage of individual liberty and democratic principles that made America's governmental system work – then and now.

It was that spirit of individual liberty that prompted Thomas Paine to say: "That government is best which governs least." Americans have so firmly believed in the principle ever since that it is hard to imagine this country in any other light. The idea that we have a right to live our lives without government interference in day-to-day affairs is what the Revolution was all about – regardless of whether the government involved was English or American – or local. But this innate feeling has run up against a modern problem that is causing a good deal of distress.

For the last several generations, Americans have been asking their governments – at all levels – to do more and more for them. We take for granted – and insist upon – good roads, clean water,

effective sanitation, crime control, legal protection, fairness in economic dealings, and a host of other endeavors. We tend to forget,
or would like to ignore, that all these things come at a price – and
not just an economic price. Even in its most benign postures, government must determine certain things about us. [Are we old
enough and skilled enough to drive a car? How many of us live in
our state and city? And so forth.]

Bitter complaints about government intrusion in our lives and
high taxes are misguided. They arise from unrealistic expectations about modern life, considering what we continually ask for.
They are wishes to get something for nothing, which is not really
the American way. Discussions are needed to clearly focus on
ways America's government and citizens can improve the country
and its prospects for the future. So let's begin.

A "More Perfect Union"

The Preamble to the US Constitution: *"We the People of the
United States, in Order to form a more perfect Union, establish
Justice, insure domestic Tranquility, provide for the common de-
fence, promote the general Welfare, and secure the Blessings of
Liberty to ourselves and our Posterity, do ordain and establish this
Constitution for the United States of America."*

The term "more perfect Union" refers to the 1780's desire across
the new country to improve on the dysfunctional central government brought about by America's first attempt – the "Articles of
Confederation". Under those original premises, each state was a
nearly-sovereign entity unto itself. The central government was
empowered to do little more than conduct foreign affairs and fight
wars, should they become necessary. The state legislatures provided whatever funds they chose to contribute to common interests, including war making. It was clearly an unsatisfactory situation. The one-chambered Congress was the sole element of government and would delegate all powers to a "Committee of the
States" when it was itself in recess. The committee soon dissolved into factions and was a complete failure, never having seriously performed its intended function. So there was, functionally,
neither an executive nor judicial power to the government under

the Articles. The states, and chaos, reigned across the land. So another Constitutional Convention was called (with George Washington presiding) and our current constitution was written and debated at length.

During the months of 1788 while the thirteen original states held conventions to ratify or reject the US Constitution and its Preamble, George Washington pointed at least twice toward a solution we want to consider for our modern age.

In a letter to an Irish Member of Parliament discussing the state of politics and likelihood of war in Europe, he wrote: "It should be the policy of United America to administer to their wants, without being engaged in their quarrels." [Letter to Edmund Newenham, 29 August 1788]. In a letter to another friend [Benjamin Lincoln] he said: "No country upon earth ever had it more in its power to attain these blessings than United America."

Then five years later, in the shortest Inauguration speech ever given he said: "Fellow Citizens: I am again called upon by the voice of my country to execute the functions of its Chief Magistrate. When the occasion proper for it shall arrive, I shall endeavor to express the high sense I entertain of this distinguished honor, and of the confidence which has been reposed in me by the people of United America."

To be sure, during those years and at other times he probably used the term "United States of America" more frequently than "United America" to describe the country he was called upon to lead – but a question about his vision for the country does seem to present itself. Did George Washington see America as one country, indivisible, in a way that few of his peers seemed to recognize? The question may forever be a matter of conjecture. What we're going to discuss first in examining how America can improve itself is whether the idea has serious merit. Could we really achieve a "more perfect union" by more thoroughly uniting the states? Some alternatives:

CHAPTER 1 – Government

The State of Affairs
Who are we? What do we want to be?

One issue that has dogged this country since its inception is the question of whether America is one nation or a confederation of states. Our first attempt at self-governance foundered on just that point of contention. The second attempt has been much more successful, but the question still lingers, ominously hovering over our future.

The persistence of the country's original subdivisions is holding America back, restraining us from forthrightly progressing into the future. Of the world's 200 nations, only America maintains a hierarchy of governments with such rigidly structured spheres of influence. It is archaic and anachronistic. Actions will always be constrained to the lowest limit of what its many sections will permit it to do. America cannot march confidently into the future as a mob of separately-motivated individual governmental entities that only occasionally agree on any particular course of action. Unanimity of purpose is almost never achieved and some level of rancor is always voiced on every topic.

The American Civil War was the most tragic example imaginable of what can happen when one segment of the nation violently disagrees with another. One element driving that conflict was that the Constitution makes no provision for a state to withdraw from the Union once it has been accepted. America is truly indivisible – of that there is no doubt. The first proposal of this book is not to separate the states but to unite them, to merge them so completely as to eliminate any legal distinction between them.

The ultimate effect of that would be, in short, to eliminate the states altogether – but in the legal sense only. One thing notable to many people driving across the country is that there actually is an unmistakable difference between the geographic areas of America. Even at ground level, Kansas *does* look different from Nebraska. The changes may not be stark or immediately expressed at the state line, but they are there. There will always be a Kansas. There will always be a Nebraska.

1

However there are some odd situations that need adjustment. That small slice of the country lying east of the Ohio River but sandwiched up against the western border of Pennsylvania is only sixteen miles wide at its widest, stretching over sixty miles northward towards Youngtown, Ohio. Indeed, one of the four counties in the section is called "Ohio County". Do the residents of this swath regard themselves as "West Virginians"? They very likely have much more extensive economic and philosophic ties to eastern Ohio – or perhaps Pittsburgh over in Pennsylvania. The same can be said of the people living in the panhandle area of Maryland. Nestled high in the Appalachian Mountains between West Virginia and the southern border of Pennsylvania, the life and flavor of the place is much closer to West Virginia than the ocean-based living of Chesapeake Bay residents.

This topic of these panhandle dwellers is raised to illustrate the point that state boundaries drawn through historic conveniences create situations of under-representation in the government of the affected states. All governments operate by laws or ordinances – hopefully written with the best of intentions, that generally don't discriminate by name or location – or shouldn't. In the case of groups of citizens living in areas out of the "mainstream" of a state government's general concerns – they wind up being underserved.

None of America's states are uniform in character from border to border – either in geography or the nature of their populations. Talk of secession from their state occasionally rises in many local areas. In addition to the tragedy of the Civil War, at least 39 other attempts have been formally made by localities to secede from their present state governments – or the nation.

The best solution for the situation is to eliminate the states and their legislatures altogether. The Federal government has civil and criminal codes passed by Congress over the last two and a half centuries that can cover and regulate almost every aspect of life in America. Slathering on an additional layer of state laws compounds the difficulties of modern living. County and city ordinances multiply the complexities even more. Let's just drop all the layers of state and local governments and work towards our common goals as one nation.

I was born in Los Angeles more years ago than I care to divulge at this point. I was raised in that mega-metropolitan area and became used to the city form of local government. Counties were mostly just geographic groupings of cities – with a backdrop of rural, usually mountainous, areas behind them. The population and tax bases of the cities were large – and seemed sufficient to perform necessary services for their citizens. Moving to northern Virginia three and a half decades ago was instructive about how variable local governments can be. Local governments in Virginia are centered around the state's counties – and a smattering of "incorporated" towns located within them. Municipal services are generally provided at the county level. While not completely comfortable with the somewhat curious arrangement, we were able to adjust during the thirteen years we lived there. In the area of Pennsylvania where we live now, local governments are generally run on the "township" model for providing municipal services. This is unsatisfactory. A township containing industrial or commercial districts within its arbitrarily-drawn borders may have a generous tax base for providing governmental revenue, while its neighbors – sometimes literally just across the street – may be starved to provide the most basic of services. Even much-needed traffic lights are declared unaffordable luxuries on many occasions. Basic safety services such as fire departments and emergency medical transportation become charities needing fund-drive kind of support from local citizens – who quite often feel they can't afford to provide it.

A true visionary in many fields of endeavor, Thomas Jefferson often expressed his strong preference for American government to be based on a level as close to local as possible. But he also said that every generation of Americans should be expected to conduct a revolution regarding the means of their governance. It's clear at this point in history that American government at all levels deserves to be reviewed. The discussions proposed here are not meant to espouse any ideology, but rather to express how living in America can be improved on a practical level.

We are generally at liberty to travel where we like, buy what we can afford, and visit with whomever we choose – and that is exactly how Americans should always be able to live. Enjoying this freedom, most of us don't realize that through the hours of our days most aspects of daily living in this country are covered by community covenants, local ordinances, and state laws. The patchwork quilt of legalities we live in goes generally unnoticed – as long as our experiences with it are benign. There have, however, been many occasions and many people who have suffered from some of the consequences inherent in a non-uniform legal environment. When I was a child, my family used to watch the evening news on TV as hundreds of civil rights workers were beaten by police and sprayed with water cannons from their local fire departments. [Readers will, I hope, forgive my lack of deference for the "good old days" of the 1950s.] Their issue with the "authorities" was simply to obtain equal treatment under the law – and eventually by society in general. Though less strenuous these days, the struggle continues – and possibly always will on the sociological front.

One sure way to completely mitigate the legal aspect of the ongoing travesty would be to "nationalize" all governmental structures from top to bottom. While thoroughly standardizing services provided to American citizens, the support and training provided to civil servants at all levels would be greatly improved. Career progressions could be established that would also create an improved sense of public service for government employees at every level. Political patronage would either disappear completely or be subjected to periodic "cleansing" scrutiny of a standard rigor. Public service is an honorable life. When more thoroughly disconnected from the interference of politics, its professionals will be able to provide better governmental services for all citizens.

Why do this? What could we expect to gain?

In a word – money. Most state and local governments across America are financially destitute and are quickly approaching points where they can't borrow any more money to continue providing even the most basic of services. All possible avenues of potential efficiencies in government must be explored.

Thirty years ago a fallacy of public financing was broadcast throughout the land. It is still subscribed to by citizens who look only to the weight of their own wallets when deciding for themselves what services governments should provide. Tax levies of

4

all kinds were shredded without regard to what services would be adversely impacted. Borrowing to continue operations was encouraged because a majority of voters continued to erroneously believe that a future prosperity could be taxed (at even lower rates) by governments to repay for their current operations. That prosperity never materialized because the basic concept of "lower taxes mean more business" only works in limited contexts, for short periods. That hoped-for prosperity is now receding into the distance ahead at an accelerated pace – brought about the very borrowing that claimed it as a birth right. Later we'll discuss what should be done to solve issues of taxation in America.

So we are brought to a point in history when even improbable solutions should be examined and weighed for feasibility and impact. Let's begin:

How should the states be changed?

Option 1: Completely dissolved.

This would eliminate all functioning reference whatever to the jurisdictions currently known as "states" or "commonwealths". All governmental services would be provided in a "single tier" approach directly to American citizens without regard to where they reside within the borders of the country. Social Security payments and Veterans Affairs services have been provided this way for decades. Though some veterans might disagree due to their personal experiences with the VA bureaucracy, this actually maximizes the level of benefits received in comparison to the costs incurred.

Elimination of all individual state functions would cut out a large class of "middlemen", many of whom have been very poorly serving their constituents for generations. It would also eliminate inequalities in services provided – sometimes intentional, as noted in the above comments on America's civil rights struggles. The nearly-incredible expenditures required to support the legislative and executive branches of fifty state-level governments would no longer be necessary. The associated costs of the political campaigns waged to capture those thousands of quasi-professional posts would also no longer be required. The state- and local-level organizations currently administering government services could be incorporated into their national-level counterparts almost seamlessly.

Option 2: Administratively dissolved.

This would eliminate separate functioning of the state and commonwealth governments while retaining their geographic and administrative titles. The governors' offices and their subordinate administrations would keep those labels but rather than being elected or politically appointed, they would be established and managed by a National Civil Service Administration. The legislatures would be disbanded and their capital buildings converted into museums and libraries.

Each governor (still elected by the state's residents under this option) would be responsible for executing laws (now all national) within the boundaries of his / her district. The structures of state-level administrations would be standardized and streamlined as much as possible, with possible tailoring to suit the needs of the population in those geographic areas. State lines might be adjusted in some situations (as noted in the "panhandle" description above) to enhance convenient administration. Some larger states might even be separated into smaller, more cohesive, regional districts.

Either this option or the one just above could enable the absorption of our Pacific (Guam and Marshall Islands) and Atlantic (Puerto Rico and Virgin Island) territories fully into America's political and economic mainstream.

Option 3: Not dissolved, but changed legislatively.

Unicameral legislatures. Among the fifty states and commonwealths only Nebraska has taken the truly economical step to unify its legislative function into one body of elected delegates. In the election of 1934 the state's voters adopted a constitutional measure that eliminated the waste inherent in having two separate groups to pass their laws. While tempted to quantify the governmental savings they have achieved over the decades since, in this book we'll just admire the wisdom of the achievement. The potential for savings is obvious. When a bill is passed by the one authorized legislative body, no effort to compromise with a second group is necessary. The bill goes straight to the Governor's desk for signature or veto. The current bicameral structure of the other 49 legislatures around the country is simply an effort to mimic that of the Federal Congress. This copy-cat approach to state-level government is incredibly wasteful and useless. It isn't often repeated, thankfully, at the local level and should be abolished by states with due dispatch all across the nation.

Option 4: Fully Integrate All US Territories into the Country.

During the westward sweep of American government across the continent, the territories that eventually became states passed through phases of administrative limbo known as "incorporated organized territory" (meaning they were intended to become states) and "unincorporated organized territory". American Samoa, Guam, Northern Mariana Islands, Puerto Rico, US Virgin Islands, and Wake Island are considered in the second (and truly second-class) condition. We have over four million citizens living in these under-served areas of the nation. It is well documented that they all have higher rates of poverty and lower rates of all the civil services that Americans enjoy across the rest of the country.

If Option 1 above is not taken, these territories should be integrated into the nation as states or new components of existing states. Puerto Rico and the US Virgin Islands should join the Union as the "Atlantic Islands" state and American possessions in the Pacific should be administratively annexed into Hawaii.

Necessary Changes to the Federal government

Option 1: Abolish the Senate.

The same unicameral approach to legislation should be made at the national level. The United States Senate should be abolished. It was originally proposed in 1787 as a compromise between populous states and the smaller ones, who feared domination from their larger cohorts. It has always been an elitist, non-democratic organization. Its members have been directly elected as the peoples' representatives only since 1913.

The same arguments about duplication or triplication of legislative efforts apply here. Our national government is becoming paralyzed by the requirement for exact agreement between two versions of legislative bills that might eventually be passed by either the Senate or the House of Representatives. Life in America is growing more complex every day – and its citizens are asking more of their governments all the time. The urge to satisfy those demands is fostering increasingly complex legislation – even when the original requirements are fairly simple. By the time special "riders" and pork-barrel amendments are attached to meaningful legislation, the bills become unreadable and quite often, unintelligible or downright counter-productive. Though this sorry state has other remedies to be discussed shortly, the argument made here is that elimination of the "upper" house of Congress will at least streamline the legislative function. Also, if the first option 1 above were to be adopted, the concept of "big state vs. little state" disappears. Even if the states are retained, elimination of the Senate is desirable from the standpoint of "democratizing" the legislative process. For nearly 125 years, the Senate effectively reduced the power of the average American citizen to influence the federal government. After 1913, direct election of Senators improved that situation in theory but the elitism inherent in such a "house of lords" is still basically anti-thematic to the American way of life.

Should the Senate be abolished, the House of Representatives could establish Select Committees to perform the two primary Constitutional functions of the Senate – treaty ratification and vetting of Presidential appointments.

Option 2: Keep the Senate, but detach it from law-writing.

Another way to remove the legislative obstruction of bicameralism but retain the familiar, though anachronistic, Congressional structure would be to strip the Senate of responsibility for writing law. Senators could still pass judgment on Presidential appointments and ratify treaties when required. This should dramatically improve the consideration and approval rate of Presidential appointments, which has fallen to a shockingly bad state of affairs. To otherwise occupy their time, Senators could debate issues of the day in a true "house of lords" manner, without affecting necessary legislation.

Option 3: Eliminate Congressional "redistricting" by state legislatures.

Whether states and commonwealths are retained as they are now or converted into administrative districts, all Representatives should be elected on a state-wide basis [This "general ticket" approach was used by several states prior to 1842.] or by districts drawn up through a non-political technique. *"Gerrymandering" of Congressional districts MUST BE STOPPED*. Lurid stories of self-interested political manipulation of districts are historic, legendary, and scandalous. [The term "gerrymander" came into being in 1812 when the Massachusetts legislature drew up a state senate district that looked like a salamander – and the bill was signed by the governor Elbridge Gerry.]

Political scientists have devised numerous schemes for redistricting in attempts to minimize the negative effects of this corrupting process – but the best solution is just to abolish the practice entirely. There are twenty-four states which have five or fewer Congressional seats in the House of Representatives – seven of those are represented by only one member. Those states have little or no problem whatever with gerrymandering.

Selfish interests of "what can you do for me" have permeated American politics since the country's inception and the periodic redrawing of district lines is one of the primary methods used to ensure that those interests triumph over the common good. At best, representatives are overly focused on promoting the interests of their hometowns (or worse, people they've made underhanded deals with before and after election) while voters going into their booths ponder which candidate is going to do them the most good personally – or perhaps, while holding their noses, vote for the candidate they feel who will do them the least harm.

What is really needed in America, at all political levels, is a greater sense that our citizens, in and out of office, should keep an eye on what they feel is important for the country as a whole, not just their own pockets or neighborhoods. Consolidating all of a state's Congressional districts into one and voting for representation from a slate of candidates would go a long way toward achieving that higher purpose.

If political districts are to be retained, a non-political solution to the gerrymandering problem must be used. Fortunately, one has already been developed – by the telephone industry. Telephone area codes mimic population patterns reasonably well, don't cross state boundaries as of yet, and could be used as basic guidelines for drawing up Congressional district boundaries and determining Electoral College representation. If the state-wide method of Congressional elections is not adopted, this alternative method should be taken up as soon as possible. Another non-political parsing of the country could be achieved through use of postal zip codes to define Congressional districts.

Option 4: Term Limits – Really.

A. Presidential: Until Franklin Roosevelt was elected to serve as President four times (1932, 1936, 1940, 1944), no one deemed it necessary to establish a limit on how many times the same individual might serve as President, since they all had deferred to George Washington's judgment that "two terms was enough". Within two years of Roosevelt's death in office, the twenty-second Amendment to the Constitution was proposed and it became effective in 1951. This situation can be improved still further. To reduce the influence of politics on incumbents, presidential stints in office should limited to one six year term. That will provide enough time for Presidents to enjoy (or suffer from) the fruits of their labors – without undue concern for their re-election prospects. They would be free to more directly focus on their primary job of leading the country and directing the affairs of Government, not the politics of trying to double their own tenure in office.

B. <u>Congressional</u>: If the Senate still exists, limit the Senators' service to three six year terms – elected on the same rotational basis as currently. Representatives should be allowed to serve in the House for a maximum of four four-year terms with half of them elected during each two-year election cycle. This would free up more of their time to actually get legislation passed rather than garnering political and financial support for the currently too-frequent election process.

C. <u>Judicial</u>: Supreme Court Justices should be retired after 18 years. With nine judges on the panel, a new justice would be chosen every two years. Each President would, therefore, be able to nominate three Justices during his one term in office. Though nominally non-political, the Supreme Court has always been influenced to some degree by the political winds of the day. Establishing a definite, predictable rotation in the panel will reduce the Congressional stress involved in (and hopefully accelerate) the process of vetting the appointments.

Option 5: The Electoral College.

There have been public complaints about the Presidential Electoral College ever since 1800 when Thomas Jefferson and Aaron Burr tied with equal numbers of electors and 36 ballots were needed to pick Jefferson as the new President. Matters got worse in 1824 when, during another tied-up Electoral College situation, John Quincy Adams was selected by Congress to become President after Andrew Jackson achieved a majority of citizens' votes cast nationwide. While many of the proposals in this book may be sweeping, elimination of the Electoral College is not actually among them. A simple counting of nationwide votes by any means – at any level – at whatever degree of accuracy – is simply not "official enough" to bear the Constitutional weight of selecting America's next leader. The current technique of having legislatures "validate" election results within their states and passing that on to Congress is formal enough – but wouldn't apply if the first or second proposals above were to be adopted and state legislatures were to be eliminated.

Under the second option, each state's Governor could oversee the electoral process and forward their results to Congress. But that wouldn't really solve the main complaint about the Electoral College – the distance it creates between the citizen and the selection of a President. What's needed to improve the situation is to eliminate the "block" voting aspect of the electoral balloting, wherein the presidential candidates get all or none of a state's votes.

The Congressional District Method used by Maine and Nebraska may look like an improvement, but it is still not the best solution. In this process, the presidential candidate winning in each congressional district gets one vote of the state's total, with the two senatorial votes going to the candidate winning the most of the other votes. This technique would significantly elevate the stakes involved with district "gerrymandering", which is an insidiously corrupting political practice that MUST be stopped for the reasons noted above.

So the final proposal here is that under options 2 or 3 above in the first set (those relating to the existence of states), the Governor of each state would determine by what percentages their voters preferred the Presidential candidates and then divide those electoral votes proportionately, without regard to the "extra" Senatorial votes, which would be abolished along with the Senate.

Another approach already being undertaken by twelve states (as of this printing) is to award all their electoral votes to the candidate who receives the most votes overall nationwide. The electoral vote total of these states stands at 172 at the moment. The Interstate Compact will take effect when states comprising another 98 electoral votes have passed similar laws. This is actually the best solution to the historic injustice wrought by the current status of the presidential electoral process and should be promoted among the remaining state legislatures. It would not require a Federal Constitutional amendment or even approval from Congress to accomplish.

CHAPTER 2 – Taxes

The State of Affairs

Taken in total, the federal tax codes in America are incredibly complex. Written, rewritten, and compiled over decades they are one of the principal tools through which the Federal government attempts to influence the lives and behavior of Americans, both citizens and visitors. Ostensibly dedicating itself to the principle of freedom, the Government offers tax "incentives" to bribe or cajole taxpayers into performing acts of which it approves. It also uses tax penalties to punish actions regarded as undesirable. Whether they receive the "carrot" or the "stick", Americans generally wind up feeling abused and confused by the tax system as they try to navigate their way through life.

From the earliest days of this country, taxes have been a primary motivator for action. The Shays' Rebellion against the fees levied on Revolutionary War veterans in Massachusetts prompted George Washington to favor a stronger central government and our current Constitution is one of the results. The Whiskey Rebellion during Washington's first administration was one of his biggest domestic challenges. Americans' distaste for taxes is historic [In 1794 Washington himself rode out from Philadelphia towards Pittsburgh at the head of a 13,000-man army to enforce payment of the tax.] – and also quite modern.

What's needed is to develop a broad understanding in the public mind that government IS necessary and that taxes ARE necessary to fully pay for what it is required to do. The current lack of agreement on this basic reality is disconcerting. Too many Americans get lost in the details of the arguments about this and frustrations arise among people who might otherwise be able to develop intelligent solutions. So let's try to keep things simple and realistic:

What do we want American government to do?

The four primary things that the Federal government charges itself to do are to provide National Defense, ensure Domestic

Tranquility, accomplish Public Works and perform Public Services. National Defense and Domestic Tranquility are essentials and not really subject to much debate among truly thoughtful citizens. The details of how Public Works and Services are defined and what levels of accomplishment are to be achieved is where almost all the disputes arise. The arguments are extensive and will be endless until the following basic principles are achieved: The solution to the dilemma is to determine in an orderly manner exactly what the government's public works and services to its citizens and visitors should be – and then calculate how expensive those tasks will be to accomplish. Some considerations:

Option 1: Price the Bills.

Each bill passing through Congress should be "priced" on the basis of its cost to the average taxpayer. Members of Congress would then be able to tell their constituents in dollars and cents how successful their efforts at representation have been. The Congressional Budget Office already does this for most bills. Wide publication of its results should be made a mandatory part of the legislative process. "Earmarks" on bills favoring specific regions or groups of people must be prohibited completely.

Option 2: Lengthen the Budget Cycle.

Government budgets should be developed and passed on a two-year basis instead of annually. The task requires so much effort that Congress and the President now have little time for much else and governance of the country suffers. Most federal departments already plan their work according to five-year (or longer) plans, which are priced as accurately as those made during the formal budget process. This option would cost nothing to implement while improving the governmental result significantly.

Option 3: Balance the Budgets.

All governmental budgets should be balanced between revenues received and expenditures made. Whether on an annual basis or through short-range multi-year plans, American government must not continue to accrue debt that it pushes forward for future generations to pay. This has never been fair – and never will be. The federal government has not been fully out of debt since Andrew Jackson's first administration, so it's obvious that the problem is a long-standing one – but it must end and we must start heading in the right direction now.

Option 4: Flatten the Tax Structure, Eliminate the Deductions.

From a standpoint of personal liberty, governmental efforts to control citizens' behavior through the "carrot and stick" use of tax codes is objectionable. Wealthy people and big corporations seem very adept at extracting many "carrots" from government while bitterly complaining about being whipped with the "stick". Middle-class and poor people, and small businesses, on the other hand, seem to be getting hit with the stick much more often – and to a much greater negative impact. The graduated income tax intended to "level the field" for all Americans' pursuit of happiness doesn't seem to be working very well for anyone. How could the situation be improved? Could flattening the tax structure really help at all?

In Pennsylvania where we live now, the state income tax rate is 3.2%. No exemptions or deductions influence the dollar amount paid by the Commonwealth's residents. Every tax return we file accurately matches the withholdings previously contributed to within a few cents. Whether or not the state budget is balanced is a conjecture depending on what the state legislature has decided to do with its revenues. But no one argues about whether or not the taxes paid are fair. The same principle can be applied at the federal government level – whether or not the states are dissolved.

The bottom line of the argument is simple: Unfairness in taxes arises from the complexity of the taxation process. When the Government stops trying to influence its citizens' behavior through tax codes, the atmosphere of freedom we all seek to enjoy will improve. Rich people and large corporations, having benefitted more from American society than others, do deserve to pay more than those less fortunate – whether they be individual citizens or businesses of whatever size. Having the rich pay a somewhat higher rate (as well as larger dollar amounts achieved by a truly "flat" rate) is also probably appropriate – though that does lean away from the fully "Libertarian" direction of a completely flat tax. What is unfair – and should be stopped – is the incredibly complex structure of tax exemptions, deductions, and "incentives" that have so fully corrupted the taxing process in America.

As a middle-class taxpayer my basic federal tax withholding rate is 28%. At least that is what would be taken out of my pay before the exemption process kicks in. [We claim an exemption for our home mortgage and there are pre-tax exclusions derived from our health plan participation.] At the bottom line of our tax forms every year, we usually wind up paying around 12% after going through the itemized deduction process. [Our personal exemptions are figured higher up in the 1040 Form process.] We also make use of "incentives" that may apply to what we've done to improve our home and living standards. I'm not going to be naïve enough to ignore financial savings offered to me by the governmental environment in which we live – even if I don't agree with them in theory.

However, it is very irritating to realize that the same taxation complexities that permit me to recoup 16% of my earnings also permit billionaires and large corporations to pare down their tax contributions to nearly nothing whatever. ***THIS HAS TO STOP.*** Loudly proclaimed "loophole" closures are never going to make the kind of changes America needs to establish fairness in our taxes or provide financial solvency for our government. What is needed is a basic overhaul of the taxation concept – also kept fully in view of what the government needs to do. Let's reiterate the option:

Flatten tax rates, eliminate exemptions and deductions, and <u>offer no returns</u>.

If some of the states can figure their share of citizen's earnings and deduct them without much error, the federal government can do the same. The federal workforce currently devoted to analyzing tax contributions from citizens should be redeployed to identifying income and taxable assets.

Option 5: Eliminate the Income Tax?

The income tax might be replaced by institution of other taxes such as General Sales taxes or excise taxes on certain items, products, or processes. While this might seem attractive to a populace having grown to hate the Income Tax, fairness of this proposal would depend completely on the items and processes chosen to be taxed and the levels of taxation determined to be appropriate. The effects would be completely unpredictable and capricious in terms of supporting the requirements of government and society.

The ancient Eastern concept of "Karma" is based on souls "reaping what is sown" – meaning that their past actions cause or influence the things that happen to them later. One of the principal venues of this rigorous spiritual accounting is food consumption. (You are what you eat – and perhaps you become what you eat.) In a similar manner, all free citizens have a financial income of some sort. So at the bottom line, an Income Tax is really the fairest way to provide revenue for a government that attempts to support all of its citizens.

So as a last word on taxes, options one through four should be adopted. The tax rates citizens are asked to pay should be determined as fairly as possible – in comparison to the requirements that the citizens demand from their government.

That means that we must determine for ourselves as a nation what we want our society to be. Do we feed the hungry? Do we provide a home to the homeless? Do we protect elder citizens from the ravages of sickness and old age? Do we protect citizens and visitors from their own foolish actions? How do we protect citizens and visitors from the foolish and criminal actions of others?

When exemptions, deductions, and returns are eliminated from the tax process the Federal Government's Internal Revenue

Service personnel will be able to devote most of their time to identification of citizens' income and ensuring that those incomes are included in the national tax base.

Option 6: Eliminate paper currency.

A thoroughly realistic action on this journey will be to eliminate paper money. The average useful lifespan of a dollar bill (and all other denominations) in general circulation is about 18 months. The useful life of America's minted coins averages 18 years. That fact alone is enough to justify the change. America should start replacing all lower denomination paper money with coins as an intermediate step on the road to elimination of all hand-held currency. Higher denominations should be phased out soon afterward in lieu of electronic transactions.

There will be a huge savings achievable when we no longer have to try to print money that is counterfeit-proof. While counterfeiting coins is also possible to accomplish – it's quite a bit more difficult to achieve and could be thoroughly prevented by embedding small radio frequency ID (RFID) chips in the coins.

Option 7: Return all "off-shore" assets held by Americans.

Much concern is raised in public discussions about how great the national debt has become. Not many Americans know that the amounts of money held by their rich fellow citizens in foreign banks and other havens – primarily to avoid paying taxes – would pay off the entire national debt twice over. This practice must end. It should be punished either by complete confiscation of all such funds or by fully exercising Internal Revenue penalties for tax avoidance. This second action might not fully eliminate the national debt, but would go further to pay it down than most other options being publicly discussed.

CHAPTER 3 – Law Enforcement

The State of Affairs

Across America, there are 3,077 county governments when 42 cities in various states and the District of Columbia are considered as distinct legal entities on that level. Though many cities have their own Municipal Courts, the primary practice and enforcement of Law in America is expressed at the county level. County Boards of Supervisors are charged with overseeing affairs in their geographic districts but most operate in obscurity with little more to do than to try to maintain roadways and provide basic water and sewer services. The most visible sign of county and other local governments, when they are visible, are law enforcement personnel. Generally well-trained in the performance of their duties, they are often outmanned and outgunned by some of the lower elements of society that travel through, or hide themselves in, their limited jurisdictions.

The most acute awareness most Americans maintain of local law enforcement personnel is watching for "speed traps" as they drive along the highways. Criminals traveling the roads often have a distinct advantage over the local officers because of the totally fractured detection and enforcement system of justice across the country.

If a local tough guy punches a bobby in the nose in Manchester, England, they'll know about it at Scotland Yard within the hour. If someone robbing a bank in Illinois can get over the county line without a hot pursuit, he'll have several extra hours or a whole day to get further away or hide completely from view until his next robbery. This localization of law enforcement in America is completely anachronistic and must be eliminated from our modern society.

A long-standing travesty exists in America with regard to our failed attempts to eliminate use of intoxicating substances for recreational purposes. Much of the over-crowding in the nation's prison system is the result of legally persecuting otherwise law-abiding citizens because they consume substances that the government at some jurisdictional level has decided should be prohibited. This must cease immediately for the good of the nation and all its citizens, whether or not they consume these substances. Here are some recommendations on improving America's law enforcement environment:

Option 1: Unify Law Enforcement on a National Level.

Establish one code of justice across America, both criminal and civil. Review existing U.S. Codes and streamline them for effective deployment across the country. These should supersede (meaning replace) all state laws and local ordinances. Nationalize all law enforcement officers and standardize their training, pay, facilities, and support equipment. Unify the judicial system into one national structure. Combine or interface all police computer databases and criminal tracking techniques.

Option 2: Modernize Detection Techniques.

The most effective scientific techniques of evidence review and criminal identification should be employed in all criminal cases. DNA and other scientifically verifiable methods should be used to identify suspects and positively prove innocence or guilt. Extracting confessions through lengthy interrogation sessions should be eliminated. Even voluntary confessions should be regarded as invalid unless they can be verified by concrete evidence independently developed by police personnel.

Option 3: Build More Prisons.

Ask almost any professional detention officer and they'll tell you there are two fallacies of the American criminal system: deterrence and rehabilitation. The threat of doing prison time deters very few criminals from their first (or next) criminal act because they don't expect to get caught. Few inmates ever positively change their outlook on life because of prison experience and fewer still learn non-criminal skills that will help prevent them from returning to a life behind bars.

The widely-practiced process of prison parole should be abandoned nationwide. It serves no purpose except to reduce criminals' disincentive to commit crimes. Paroles granted early to ease overcrowding in prisons does a disservice to the criminals' victims and society as a whole, particularly when the felons are unleashed to commit further crimes -- sometimes against the same victims whom they blame for their incarceration.

There is no doubt that some prison systems are so over-crowded that residing within their walls constitutes "cruel and un-usual punishment". Releasing offenders early, however, is a jour-ney in the wrong direction. Building as many prisons as necessary to humanely house all criminals through their full sentences is the proper solution to these and many other problems of the judicial system.

Option 4: Two Strikes and You're Out.

Waiting for a career criminal to commit his third felonious of-fense before a non-paroled life sentence is settled upon his shoul-ders is inviting at least one more victim to join the ranks of the under-served in America. Since most criminals never expect to get caught and then to get out early if they do, gives them the perception that the gates of the prison system are little more than a "revolving door". That should be made into a "one way street" where they know for certain that they should "abandon all hope" of returning to the open and free society that they once sullied with their crimes.

Option 5: Curtail Prisoners' Access to the Internet.

Another disturbing aspect of modern society is the ease with which felons can electronically reach out between their prison bars and insert themselves into Internet transactions. With all Ameri-cans spending more time sitting in front of computer monitors to conduct daily business and entertain themselves, the distinction between life "on the outside" and their incarceration starts to blur for many criminals. Where is the punishment when a criminal is not deprived of a pursuit in which he or she would be engaged if not behind bars?

The material mischief these individuals can create while elec-tronically pretending to be regular citizens must be completely pre-vented. This can be done by ensuring that they have absolutely no electronic transaction capability other than initiating educational pursuits or honest vocational training for themselves.

Option 6: NEVER Release Pedophiles or Sexually-Addicted Criminals.

One of the truly saddest aspects of modern life is sexually-based criminal behavior – particularly crimes perpetrated against children, followed closely by violent sex crimes against women. A growing number of the people committing these crimes publicly admit that they will never stop perpetrating their travesties as long they are provided opportunity. Some few among them even reluctantly plead to not be released into society. That fate must be granted to all of them – after the first definitively-proven offense. To date, no psychological measures ever developed appear to be truly effective in deterring these individuals from repeating their offenses, which often escalate into truly horrendous acts. While society may not be able to definitively detect prospective aberrational behavior, we can at least prevent repetition by the same individuals by never letting them out prison.

Option 7: Sexual Assault and Sexual Harassment

Sexual assault (defined as unwanted sexual touching) and the harassment that often precedes it must be fully recognized and appropriately punished immediately – in every single proven case. Every perpetrator who escapes swift justice will continue to prowl their local environment or troll the Internet looking for further victims to pursue and violate. Sexual assault can proceed toward true rape in mere seconds – and can often lead to violence toward and death of the hapless victim. The best way to eliminate this horrific circumstance is to appropriately recognize the vile behavior in early stages and to get potential perpetrators to stop committing these crimes before they start.

Option 8: A Change for Family Law – Give the Property to the Children.

Another distressing thing to observe in modern American life is the degradation of living standards for children of divorce. Through no fault of their own children of divorcing parents are often forced to shuttle between the homes or temporary dwellings of the two people they still love, who have decided to live apart – often for reasons they don't understand. The tired old phrase that "it's really the children who suffer most" is precisely true – and the most unfair. Family Court judges know this and they often struggle with custody decisions that would give Solomon a migraine.

These choices could be simplified substantially in most cases by simply awarding the family home (whatever that may be) to the children and force the parents to find alternative living accommodations according to their means, decided in other aspects of the divorce decree. The former spouse could use the family the dwelling for his or her period of custody only – removing to their separate residence when their time with the children has expired. In some cases, the divorced parents might even work out arrangements to share the one alternate living site between them.

Option 9: Replace Highway Speed Traps With Electronic Velocity Measurement of Vehicles.

An onerous and occasionally dangerous duty performed by local and state law enforcement personnel forces them to wait in their semi-hidden vehicles to snare unwary speeding motorists passing too quickly through their jurisdictions. This is an incredible waste of the uniformed officers' time. It is also ineffective because most drivers who drive too fast don't get caught most of the time they're violating the speed laws.

The solution to this is to have active Radio Frequency Identification Devices (RFIDs) mandatorily placed in vehicles that will monitor how frequently, and for what durations of time, the driver of each vehicle is driving above posted speed limits. Each vehicle's registered owner could then be taxed an amount appropriate to the level of violations that are electronically determined.

With punishment being thusly assured, compliance with speed laws would be greatly increased and the dangers to officers and civilians would be greatly reduced.

With the elimination of state and local governmental variations proposed above, uniform standards of speed limits could be applied nationwide. Speed limits would be determined by standardized application of scientific safety principles to local conditions. (If the road has a curve of a certain sharpness or a certain grade of declination, the speed limit would be set by formula, etc.)

Insurance companies are already contemplating the idea of tracking their customers' driving speed – offering premium rate discounts to their safer drivers. All that would be necessary is for creation of federal (or state, if they still exist) regulations permitting insurance companies to punitively charge their customers who routinely drive too fast. Increased profits resulting from the change could be passed, in whole or in part, to the legal jurisdictions where the violations occurred. This "speed tax" could be used to repair and improve the highways over which the violators drive – or for other governmental purposes.

Option 10: Adopt a Rational Approach To Recreational Drug Use.

America has two drugs of historical significance – alcohol and nicotine. In Washington DC, images of tobacco flowers festoon the Capitol building in many of its public areas. As noted above, George Washington's greatest domestic challenge as President was a revolt over alcohol commerce in western Pennsylvania. At all levels, American government should adopt policies that freely permit use of any substance that is less dangerous – in its usual mode of consumption – than alcohol. Anyone so inclined can kill themselves at one sitting with a large enough bottle of liquor. No one has ever "smoked themselves to death" with any burnable substance that didn't ignite their clothing.

CHAPTER 4 – Education

The State of Affairs

The future prospects of every nation rest on the welfare and well-being of its children. Every human being is born as a blank slate where the lessons of the past can be inscribed and future actions can be molded. Every child's living years are shaped by the education that Life provides them. War-torn nations and failed states provide little to learn except inhuman wildness, fear, and a selfish tyranny of the soul that leads toward personal impoverishment. The ladder of Civilization that Mankind climbs is marked at every rung by the success achieved in training young minds to respect the lessons of the past and work toward a hopeful future of Peace and Prosperity for all.

While learning is a natural function of human life and therefore comparatively effortless, assimilating the organized instruction required during an education is work – something that might not be universally achieved in a society. The desirability of having their populace educated has inspired leaders from Plato, the Talmud writers, the Aztecs, and Martin Luther to establish or recommend compulsory education for children in their societies. Modern efforts in America are modeled after the educational system established by Prussian King Frederick II in 1763. Though many of America's "Founding Fathers" were "home schooled", so to speak, they recognized the value of setting up public education for all prospective citizens. Starting with Massachusetts in 1852 and going on through to Mississippi in 1918, all states established compulsory education for young Americans.

Current estimates are that 88% of American children in school are in public schools, with 9% in religious schools, 1% in "independent" schools, and 2% being "home schooled". Heated debates have been going on for many years about which of these environments provides the better education. The arguments are very likely to be endless – with no consensus ever achieved, but they all miss the substantive point.

The real issue is that, for different reasons pertaining to each, all four techniques generally fail at providing the quality of education that our students need. There are many signs that America is failing to teach enough young people the full range of scholastic and practical curricula that will carry the nation forward through the 21st century. In international comparisons, the overall performance of America's students after completing their educational careers is abysmal. Comparisons made between Americans and citizens of other industrialized nations well after schooling shows the same trends – so our failure to educate is long-term and historic. This is truly regrettable but it is something that can be changed. It MUST be changed. Without citing the failings of the four methods we'll just go on to recommendations for correcting the situation.

Option 1: Establish a National Curriculum.

The basic educational subjects of Science; Math; English; Social Studies; and Physical Education must be presented to all students in a manner that is balanced for their ages and skill levels. Commonly offered electives such as Computers; Athletics; Career and Technical Education, Performing Arts, Foreign Languages, and Junior Reserve Officer Training should also be offered to all students as their own interests dictate.

Educational materials necessary to fully complete the national curriculum should be made available on the Internet to all institutions and individuals licensed to provide it. For "home schooling" this means that parents or guardians choosing that option must register themselves as private educators, specifying the names, ages, and residences of the children they intend to teach.

Option 2: Eliminate Textbooks, Distribute Educational Materi als Electronically.

School districts across the country are realizing that electronic methods of text presentation are now less expensive than traditional text books – and do not require periodic replacement. They are also less physically stressful for students to carry between classes and from school to home. They should be adopted nationwide immediately.

Option 3: Electronically Post Students' Results and Educational Progress.

All student testing should be performed electronically in every classroom. Scoring for physical education and performing arts achievements for their students could be posted in the national records by instructors. Both scholastic and physical education achievements for "home schooled" students would be measured through periodic assessments performed by their local school, at the school. Home-schooled students not meeting basic standard minimum achievements would be ushered into the public school system after the first time they fail an appellate examination.

Option 4: Federally Fund All Educational Institutions.

All education funding should be provided by the Federal Government. Education is a national issue of great importance. Local, state, and private entities have shown themselves to be unable to adequately provide the educational services necessary for American children. Cost is the most frequently cited reason for the failure to provide those services. This option will eliminate that obstacle. Citizens desiring to give their children education "privately" – whether through parochial or independent schools, or by personal effort – would not be excused from paying the taxes necessary to support the public school system. Those schools would receive funding commensurate to support the number of children registered – at the public school level of support. Any additional costs would be borne by those schools' endowments or the parents electing to take those options. Parents opting to "home school" could be provided the electronic equipment necessary for their registered children.

Option 5: Nationally Standardize School Administrations.

School administrators, teachers, and all other supporting personnel should be incorporated into a national structure of professional educators. Whether or not they formally become part of the Federal Civil Service, their performance standards and measurement of achievements should be standardized nationally. This will establish a fully functioning career progression in education wherein no teacher or administrator needs to shade their decisions with regard to local feelings about educational materials or processes.

Option 6: Routinely Extend the Education Process Through College.

Not everyone needs, or wants to get, a full four-year or higher college degree. But Americans must realize that in general, their lifetime earnings increase with every year of formal education they get. Someone can lose a job – or even, Heaven forbid, lose a family member – but an education gained is a treasure that they always retain regardless of whatever else may happen to them in life. America must begin to routinely offer and provide support for its citizens to extend their educations as far as the individual may desire.

To those who might say that adopting these recommendations would destroy Americans' freedom of choice in education – the argument must be raised that what they propose is retaining the freedom to fail. America's education system is failing miserably. It is not coming close to what we need to maintain our preeminent place in world society. Our nation's future depends on how we educate ourselves and our children. These changes must be discussed and hopefully accepted as a reasonable course of action to achieve what we must accomplish in educating ourselves and our precious children.

CHAPTER 5 – Immigration

The State of Affairs

An eloquent statement of America's announced hope for the world is on a plaque that was placed on the pedestal of the Statue of Liberty in 1912, twenty-six years after the statue itself was dedicated in 1886:

> Give me your tired, your poor,
> Your huddled masses yearning to breathe free,
> The wretched refuse of your teeming shore.
> Send these, the homeless, tempest-tossed to me,
> I lift my lamp beside the golden door!
> [Emma Lazarus, 1883]

The unspoken irony here is that the period of the statue's creation and the dedication of this theme to it was the very time in America's history when we were slamming shut the door to the unrestricted immigration that created this country and made it great. The namesakes of my family came to America while the Constitution was being debated in thirteen statehouses across the small nation running along the Atlantic coast. There were no Immigration Service bureaucrats down at the Baltimore dock in 1788 to inspect their dentition or quarantine their baggage.

The great Nineteenth Century expansion of America was largely powered by Europeans of all economic classes pouring onto our eastern shores and eventually met by Asians streaming into Pacific ports from the Orient. Africans finally freed from centuries of bondage in 1865 also lent their efforts to advance the national cause of showing the world that Democracy can work when liberally watered with the nutrients of Freedom and Liberty.

Many modern Americans like to think back wistfully about their hopeful forebears looking up at the statue while they passed by on their way to Ellis Island. This was the prison where they were interred before being judged to be fit residents – and perhaps future citizens of America. This ironic travesty was imposed on European immigrants by the generations of their peers who had, by sheer luck in many cases, been able to precede them. Restrictions on immigrations across the Pacific were even more severe – and more racially motivated.

Abuses perpetrated against these immigrants are celebrated by many of their modern descendants as a sort of "rite of passage" on the way to becoming Americans. It is actually a sad commentary on human nature that anyone should be made to suffer the least indignity or unfair treatment simply because they are "new" to the society they have chosen to make their home. Much of modern American history is colored (or "tainted", if you prefer) with millions of such stories – and it continues to this day.

Currently, the loud arguments over what to do about the underground nation of "illegal aliens" all miss this primary point: All members of the European-based American culture are either immigrants themselves or descended from some. The continuing prosperity of America attracts the attention and admiration of the world – and hopefully always will. All human beings able and willing to contribute to American society should be allowed to do so – whether or not they desire to remain permanently living within our borders.

Option 1: Open the Borders – Both Ways.

Immigration to America would never be "illegal" if the borders were opened to all who want to live and work here – as the founders of the country intended. The fear expressed (since the days when the Statue of Liberty was erected) by residents that immigrants are going to take too many of the available jobs is unfounded and the basic idea is just erroneous. Most unskilled newcomers settle in on the lower rungs of the economic ladder – sometimes at nearly-desperate poverty levels. They do so gladly in the belief that by the dint of their own efforts, or perhaps a little luck, they and their children will be able to climb up toward the American dream to which they aspired when they came here. The arrival of new residents increases the business base of the communities where they settle, generating new jobs for all. It is the immigration policies favoring the admission of only the "more valuable" people, such as those in place during the late 1980s, that actually undermine the higher levels of the job market for current residents. (Although the argument can be raised that these people also increase the business base and create even more jobs for individuals of all skill levels.)

Another, counter-intuitive to some people, aspect of the current situation is that "illegal" immigrants here are trapped within our borders. All people have a natural desire to return to, or at least temporarily revisit, their native land and culture. We have millions of people living in "limbo" within our borders, unable to return to or visit the families and friends they left behind, which many of them would like to do – if they were able to return unimpeded to their livelihoods in America. They hide from authorities and run with no provocation, they're afraid to have their children educated or medically treated, and become victimized by many of the denizens of the ghettos into which they force themselves. No matter how they came to reside here or whatever their legal status, they deserve better.

Those immigrants desiring to obtain American citizenship should be allowed to do so using the current naturalization processes – without being arbitrarily forced to "the back of the line". Those desiring to live and work here without becoming citizens should be granted a reviewable and renewable "guest worker" status. Immigrants should be granted a specified amount of "probationary" time to find work suitable to their skills, which might vary depending on the fields involved. To reduce the possible propensity for criminal activity, if they refuse or are unable to find such employment and don't have financial means sufficient to support themselves and their families, they should be escorted out of the country according to current practices.

Option 2: Increase Technology at Border / Entry Stations.

The usual civil liberties Americans take for granted do not apply at our borders and other points of entry. Customs and border patrol agents routinely inspect luggage, vehicle trunks, and occasionally the physical bodies of persons requesting admission to the country. This should continue – at an even more thorough level of proficiency. Facial recognition programming and computer database technology have reached a point where every person presenting themselves for entry can be screened against visual rosters of known criminals on an international basis. Those identified as such should be immediately escorted to detention and trial by the appropriate claimant jurisdictions.

Cargo entering the country at any port or other landing point MUST be thoroughly scanned by whatever means necessary to ensure contraband and other dangerous substances do not enter the country without permission. Smuggling of human beings through cargo sites should result in impoundment and permanent confiscation of the vessels involved. The corporate heads of such shipping companies should be made personally liable for the actions of the organizations under their control. Arrest warrants should posted for them so that they would be detained for trial when found here or if they attempt to enter the country at some future time.

Option 3: Block Attempted Entry at Other Points.

With the borders opened for now-legal immigration at designated entry points, anyone attempting to "cross the line" at other geographic locations will be doing so with implied nefarious intent. Such perpetrators should be immediately detained and bound over for summary trial in federal court. The ability to demonstrate accidental or otherwise unintended entry would be required to avoid conviction.

Motion detection and night-vision equipment is now sufficiently inexpensive to establish a "technological fence" to deter criminal entry, particularly after legal immigration procedures are instituted at the designated entry points and the nightly swarm of refugees and economically-desperate migrants has been curtailed.

Option 4: Eliminate "Bi-Lingual" Education.

The goal of immigration to America has always been assimilation, not differentiation. Recognition of the country's cultural diversity is well-meaning and well-founded. It should continue as a celebration – but not as a basis of business or governmental operations. We must ensure that everyone at trial or dealing with the Government understands the proceedings for or against them, but otherwise all business should be conducted in the American version of English wherever possible – even commercially. While whole-heartedly welcoming the arrival or visitation of people from the world's other 200 countries, it should be firmly recognized by all that, first and foremost, we have one unified cultural experience of being Americans. Understanding the basics of the American version of English must be considered an ultimate goal toward which all voting citizens must aspire – though lack of such proficiency should never be used to bar anyone from attaining full citizenship.

Option 5: Emphasize National Assimilation.

The above comment on using American English as a unifying influence also extends to the exercise of religious practices. There are many areas of the world – with large numbers of inhabitants – where truly abhorrent customs are practiced. America was founded on a basic principle of religious tolerance – which must always be rigorously enforced.

Every century of world history is crammed with examples of brutalities inflicted in the name of religion. Even members of the same family perpetrate the worst crimes imaginable against each other in the name of customs that are unacceptable in America. Intolerance of other faiths and other sects of the same faith are also rampant around the world today – as they always have been.

All of this MUST CEASE AT OUR NATIONAL BORDER!!

As Americans we should feel free to celebrate the diversity that makes this country great – and leave behind us the divisions that diminish all of us as human beings.

CHAPTER 6 – Guns: Control? Freedom? Right?

The State of Affairs

Ever since Europeans landed at Jamestown in 1607, firearms have been a major part of American life. Gunpowder and the lead balls their muskets propelled were the primary advantage that the small groups of European settlers had against the larger Native American populations they encountered on the frontier. At the beginning, that "frontier" was all around them. In Virginia, the Powhatan Confederacy of tribes was in a precarious circumstance when the white colonists unwelcomely arrived on their already over-populated shore. There was no miraculous "New World bounty" for them to share with the strangers and tensions rose immediately between the two groups. During the entire colonial period and beyond, Americans were disposed to carry lethal protection with them wherever they went. Back in Europe, the situation was utterly contrary. Unless actively participating in authorized warfare, most people were forbidden to own anything more weapon-like than kitchen utensils.

During the latter part of the American colonial period, British attempts to constrain the residents' urges toward freedom and independence very often involved trying to control the availability of guns and ammunition. The framers of the Constitution remembered this very well when they consciously inserted the Second Amendment into the Bill of Rights. In recent years many heated discussions have revolved around its wording – as people try to discern, in a rather nit-picking fashion, what they meant. Do Americans have an innate right to own and use firearms as they see fit? Does the Government have a right to restrict access to guns? If so, which guns? How many guns are too many for one individual to own?

The arguments will be endless – as long as we try to circumscribe modern life by the attributes of America in the 1790s. When the Second Amendment was passed every gun was a muzzle-loader. Each firearm was a hand-crafted mechanism – almost a work of art unto itself. During the early 1800s, the revolution sparked by interchangeable parts and standardized manufacturing propelled the advancement of firearms technology because Americans had a constant need for weapons that were better than their adversaries – whether Native Americans in the forests and plains or pirates on the high seas. No debate was contemplated about the rights of gun ownership when an individual's survival might depend on it while living in a hostile environment. The arguments started when America's landscape became tamed and safe enough to reasonably expect survival without the constant accompaniment of firearms. That is the common circumstance in this age so the debate rages on – rising in heat after every assassination or massive atrocity involving guns. Clearly, something must be done – but what?

Option 1: Outlaw and Confiscate All Firearms.

My deepest regret and sympathy is expressed to every parent who has lost a child or anyone who has lost an innocent family member to gun violence. The ease with which someone shouldering a rifle or holding a handgun can snuff out the lives of others is fearsome, indeed. The god-like ability to destroy life, limb, and property within sight range borders on a sick pornography. Somewhere deep in the psyche of anyone who has ever held a loaded gun, that dark thought has crept through the shadows of their mind – of that there can be little doubt.

But the complete elimination of privately-held firearms will never be achieved in this or any other nation or culture. The genie of gunpowder escaped from its bottle several centuries ago and will not be restrained again – unless basic human nature changes in a way not currently suspected as possible.

Option 2: Register All Firearms.

This *IS* a viable prospect that will help further and advance American civilization in the future. Organizations and individuals firmly committed to gun freedom must be made to understand that the Second Amendment was intended to FOSTER gun registration, not proscribe it. Law enforcement personnel have a right to know the whereabouts of lethal firearms within their jurisdictions.

By legitimizing the ownership of lawful firearms, the Constitution ensured that law enforcement personnel must allow it. But to help ensure their own safety, THEY have a basic right to know where the guns are and who holds them. As the largest and most effective organization favoring firearms, the National Rifle Association (NRA) should adopt this viewpoint and strongly support a nationwide registration program, both within and outside the ranks of its membership.

Option 3: It's Bullets, Not Guns, That Kill People. So Let's Control Them.

I once asked an NRA member who volunteered his time as a gun safety instructor whether his Second Amendment right to keep and bear firearms would be infringed if he had to make his own bullets rather than buy them by the box at the local sporting goods store. After giving the matter a bit of thought he replied that his gun rights would not really be violated. He thought it would be an inconvenience, but not a violation of his gun rights. So here is the solution:

Eliminate the public sale of manufactured ammunition. Only police organizations and active military units should be allowed to acquire, carry, and use live rounds of manufactured ammunition – as specifically related to their official functions. Police and military personnel would not be permitted use of industrially-manufactured rounds in their personal lives.

Hand-operated bullet-making equipment and supplies could be sold to individuals at the same establishments that now sell ammunition by the boxful and crate load. The skill level required for making bullets is not high but must be consistently applied. Laziness or inattention in the performance of the task is dangerous. The requirement to "roll your own" bullets will thoroughly reduce the prevalence of guns on the streets of many inner cities and other crime-ridden areas.

Registration of gunpowder purchases would be required. Small cans of gunpowder could be hermetically sealed at the factory, but have an oxidizer added that would render the powder inert six weeks after exposure to air. This would prevent individuals or criminal organizations from amassing large quantities of home-made ammunition. The possession, sale, or manufacture of non-oxidizing gunpowder in bulk form could be criminalized.

An argument could be raised that this would establish a thriving "black market" in bullets and gunpowder across the country. The counter-argument is that, on this topic – a black market is still better than an open market. The effect of these changes would probably not be felt for many years because of the billions of bullets already out in public use – but at least it would be a start down the right road.

CHAPTER 7 – Environmental Planning

The State of Affairs

Since the latter years of the 20th century, the specter of Global Warming has arisen in the public consciousness of all civilized societies. International efforts of scientists have confirmed beyond doubt that measureable increases of atmospheric energy are upon us.

A explanation should be provided here for people uninformed enough to look out their window on a snowy day and assert that global warming can't be real. In the physical science of Thermodynamics the term "warming" means an increased level of energy, not necessarily just a rise of temperature. Temperature, simply put, is the most commonly-used term to express what is actually the average speed of atmospheric molecules.

So the impact of global warming on the planet is this: More storms, stronger storms, and longer storm seasons. This includes nastier blizzards during the winter months, though they may eventually be fewer in number (both the months and blizzards) once we're further down the road to what most people will regard as a series of catastrophic disasters.

The annual number and strength of monsoonal storms experienced around the world are increasing. These storms feed voraciously on the higher temperatures of the ocean waters over which they travel and they routinely slam into our coastlines with devastating force. Even the deserts of the American Southwest now more regularly have to contend with flash flooding from storms coming off the Atlantic and Pacific coasts. At this point in time, we're at least two decades too late to actually prevent or reverse the effects of global warming on the overall world environment.

My personal feeling is that the devil's bargain was sealed when large amounts of methane gas started seeping out of the Arctic tundra in North America and Siberia. It is a process, already begun, that we will not be able to stop.

So what we'll discuss are some accommodations that America and the rest of the world must begin to make:

Option 1: Start Planning Now for a Worldwide Rise in Sea Levels.

When the ice sheet over Greenland melts completely during the next two centuries, the world's sea levels will rise by approximately twenty-one feet. When the glaciers and ice on western Antarctica melt during this century and the next, that will add another eighteen feet or so to the oceans' levels. After the immense 2-mile thick ice sheet covering eastern Antarctica melts over the next millennium, the oceans will rise some 185 feet higher yet. Though complete melting of that sheet will take some number of centuries to complete, it has happened before and appears to be beginning again. No one knows how fast the melting will be.

So in short, any coastal-facing area with an elevation less than 240 feet will at some future point be beachfront, and then undersea, property. For America, that means that almost all of New Jersey (mean elevation: 250 feet), Delaware (60 feet), Florida (100 feet), Louisiana (100 feet), and Rhode Island (150 feet) will eventually go under the waves. This will also include the District of Columbia (150 feet). Most areas currently called "tidewater" will be underwater. What is today called "piedmont" will be the new tidewater. A glance at fourth grade geography books (where the eastern US "fall line" is sometimes discussed) will give a good idea of where the new shorelines will be on the eastern shore of the country. On the west coast America's topography is more varied, but the effect will be the same. Major parts of all coastal cities will be inundated, slowly.

To be sure, breakwaters and dykes will be used for some time to "hold back the tide" but in the end the efforts will be useless. Businesses and governments should realize that their future prosperity will be found on higher ground. New Orleans, already under threat, and other low-lying river cities (such as Washington DC and Montreal, Canada) should be moved upstream or upslope in their entirety. [The nation's capital should eventually be moved to Denver anyway, to take advantage of its more central location as well as the higher elevation.]

As we retreat from the coastlines, monsoonal damage can be restrained substantially by planting thick lines of mangrove trees along the beaches at the high tide lines. Debris from storm-damaged structures should be removed, not rebuilt on their previous sites, as the oceans' tides come up to knock them down over the next several decades. A long standing policy should be established to declare all coastal zones to be public land upon their threatened inundation by the rising sea level. Use of the properties at lower tides should be mandated as temporary – and all structures there be made portable.

Option 2: Start Planning For More Rain, Where It Does Fall.

The nation's rivers will always be able to carry our runoff down to the sea. The problem is that since America's inception that has too often also included buildings, vehicles, sewage, and infrastructure like bridges and highways. Americans like to live and work near the water, whether oceanic or riverine. Since our rivers are most often not in flood stage, we tend to establish our cities, towns, farms, and factories in places that are endangered during the floods that will occur occasionally. Efforts to protect property (and lives) permanently placed in harm's way are wasteful and should be curtailed as much as possible. "Highest historic flood levels" are well known for all inhabited communities in those areas where rivers flow nearby. That is the lowest elevation where the permanent structures should be built. Only submersible or transportable property should allowed to rest in zones lower than that level. When the waters come up, those goods could then be evacuated to safer ground.

Option 3: Start Planning Now For Increased Desertification.

The world's deserts are increasing in size – and becoming hotter and drier at the same time. Grazing lands everywhere are losing their soils to the winds and large areas of too-dry lands no longer replenish the moisture their skies need to seed life-giving rains. The vicious cycle continues and will spread when the hotter winds of global warming dry out the lands even further. Once-arable crop lands are losing too much moisture and becoming fit for little more than growing the grasses needed for herds of increasingly restless animals. Global rain patterns are shifting,

moving the areas fit for agriculture to higher latitudes and eleva-
tions. Across the world, all nations must start planning for significant changes to their food production and distribution systems.
America should lead the way for the sake of humanity. One of
those efforts must be to relax international travel and migration
restrictions on a world-wide basis.

Option 4: Start Planning Now For Fewer Animals.

Biodiversity has seldom been more than a cocktail party discussion topic anywhere other than a few academic circles. Many
species of animals treasured by zookeepers and their friends have
already disappeared in the wild and the rate of extinctions is rapidly increasing. The rainforests of the world have already lost a
truly untold number of species that were never documented before
their last members returned to the ground they once trod or flew
over. Humans are persistently pushing into once-primeval wilder-
nesses everywhere without regard to even documenting what they
destroy. They seldom consider anything other than their own
property lines or obstacles standing in the way of full economic
development.

Most human cultures no longer subsist on hunting game but
the habitats of all wild animals are in severe decline and out in the
oceans, most of the world's fisheries are being depleted – both in
numbers of catch and the species of fish being caught. Mankind's
options regarding food supplies are dwindling rapidly. Prospects
for maintaining our food sources at existing levels are growing
worrisome. The world-wide increase of human beings, currently
projected to reach 9 billion people (from the current level of 7 billion) before starting to taper off four decades from now is going to
create further stress on any animal populations involved in supporting our food supplies.

Americans should understand that continued reliance on a
high-meat diet, particularly beef, is an incredibly poor use of the
nation's food production capacity. The grain used to feed cattle
and poultry for eventual slaughter could be used to feed several
times the same number of people if consumed directly by humans.
The waste products of the animals Americans eat and the by-

products of the slaughtering process befoul the land and eventually slide into our rivers, also fouling them. The resulting nitrates and other chemicals leached into the ecologic system spawn algal blooms in the river mouth coastal seas that deplete the waters of oxygen, causing massive die-offs of marine life that might otherwise be consumed by humans. Capturing that animal waste at its sources and converting it into fuel for electricity production is another mandatory option for our next topic.

CHAPTER 8 – Powering the Future

The State of Affairs

In future millennia the 20th Century will be remembered as the "Age of Oil". Petroleum products were known and used for a number of years earlier, but the widespread advent of the automobile in America dominated our history and spread to the rest of the world. Petroleum-based chemicals are used by cars from the front bumper to the rear taillights. There were many other industries extant throughout the century to be sure, but no one can doubt that the biggest change in the course of human civilization was brought about through the possibilities created by rapid personal transportation. All other forms of locomotion combined cannot compare with the impact created by the automotive revolution that truly took its first root in America.

Though the sizes of petroleum reserves deep in the earth are discussed in very high numbers (Newly fields discovered are usually described in billions of barrels.) we are told that oil is a limited resource which we are too-quickly consuming and the world may run out of oil within a few decades, at most. America leads the world in oil consumption, though a few other countries are becoming great consumers as well, and arguments are often made that Americans must stop using so much of this ever-more precious resource. Many Americans reply that we should just drill for more – even while acknowledging that it's getting much harder (and more dangerous) to find.

The common view of petroleum is that it is a "fossil fuel", created when its raw substance of rotting biomass was compressed into a liquid form by later-arriving overlying rocks. But some questions never asked are: "What was the animal or plant that made the fossil to begin with?"; "Where did those things live?"; "When did those things live?". Fossils of dinosaurs, mammoths, and such are routinely dug up around the world as bones, not thick black liquid. If the bones of a dinosaur who lived 65 million years ago can be found sticking up through the surface in some areas or buried maybe a few hundred feet below in others – **how long ago** did something have to die to have its remains gather in a big liquid pool more than two miles deep? **What** was alive so ago in such great numbers that it could leave behind billions of barrels of crude petroleum?

The answer is found today in the random appearances of oceanic slimes that seem at first like oil slicks, until they're discovered upon a closer look to be sludges of algae – still alive or recently dead. So petroleum's fossil heritage is finally revealed:

IT WAS ALGAE ALL ALONG!!

The implausibility of creating petroleum through simple pressure on random animal carcasses is seldom discussed anywhere, but we'll note it here. No one has ever demonstrated any truth to the commonly-held theory of petroleum creation. The importance of this should not be underestimated.

Observations of oceanic algae slicks in recent years have fostered some foresighted energy producers to investigate the obvious solution to our coming petroleum shortage. But the current dithering by those producers experimenting to find exactly which algae species to invest in should be ended in favor of full-bore production. The optimal species, or mix of several algae types, will be revealed through actual production in coming years and decades. Full scale production of petroleum through algae farming will eliminate the need for any drilling at any depth in any location. So that's why we should:

Option 1: Stop All Drilling For Oil and Start Farming Algae.

The search for oil has ventured into areas of the world where the nearly-unavoidable ecologic damage associated with drilling can reach truly catastrophic proportions. The expenses of drilling deeper and deeper, very often now in ecologically sensitive areas, are raising the costs of extraction to heights supported only by the theoretical future shortages envisioned by the old "fossil fuel" concept. ["We've gotta drill now or we won't have any oil at all in the future."] America must rapidly develop industrial operations to use algae's unique capability to turn itself into crude petroleum – and cease drilling into the ground for something we can grow at much less cost and no ecologic damage.

Option 2: Industrialize the Consumption of Fuel.

A good look at the fuels we use reveals that petroleum is not the only player in the game. Natural gas and coal are also available in abundance around the world, with very considerable reserves inside America's borders. At the heart of all three is the carbon atom. In natural gas and petroleum the carbon atoms form string-like molecules that are broken down and sorted during the refining process to make useful fuels and other chemicals. The lattice structure of carbon in coal deposits varies somewhat depending on the environmental circumstances when it was originally laid down. But the primary use we make of all three is the same – we burn them to create power.

The convenience of storing and transporting the heptane-octane length of the petroleum molecule as gasoline is what fueled the modern age – but it also brought on the challenges we face with global warming and environmental change. Using coal in vehicles has never been practical – except for 19th century applications in locomotives and ships. The minor experimentation done so far with vehicles powered by natural gas is a novelty.

The burning of all three fuels – in whatever form, creates much of the atmospheric carbon dioxide that threatens our future. All three forms of fuel should be burned in industrial settings where capture technologies have a good chance of eliminating the CO_2 emissions resulting from the fuels' conversion to electricity. Biofuels and commercial animal waste should also be burned in industrial settings where the carbon dioxide produced can be mitigated as much as possible. They must all be converted to electricity for consumption.

Option 3: Let's Go Electric At Home, Now.

As common sense reveals, distribution of natural gas to, or through, residential neighborhoods invites serious disaster. The fact that most cities of America's most populous state, California, lie over known active fault lines, also crisscrossed by pipelines full of explosively flammable gas, should give anyone pause about living, working, or visiting there. Electrical power service is already in place in nearly all locations nationwide. All residential gas lines should be shut down immediately across America – before the next big earthquake (in California) or pipeline rupture (anywhere) occurs. The existing nationwide network of gas pipelines should be used to route industrial supplies away from residences. New gas lines should be routed away from any residential or retail commercial area.

Option 4: Convert All Vehicles Into Hydrogen-burning Electric Hybrids.

Above almost everything else regarding their vehicles, Americans value performance. Recent technological advances in batteries and electric motor drives are coming close to achieving the levels of performance most Americans demand in their cars and trucks. That may be fine for our future, but from an ecological standpoint, that's not enough. Cars of the future didn't get us into our current global warming problem. Cars of the past did. Cars of the present are still contributing to the issue.

In 1800 two London experimenters demonstrated that with application of a low-voltage current, water can be broken down into its constituent elements – hydrogen and oxygen. Their experiment is repeated daily in high-school chemistry classes around the world. A number of Internet collaborators have designed changes to automotive engines that can take water from fuel tanks and perform this breakdown in fuel lines leading to their engines. This rather low-tech solution solves many problems and should be widely adopted as soon as possible. The reasons:

1. It eliminates the "carbon footprint" of all vehicles. The importance of this cannot be underestimated.
2. Hydrogen "packs a punch" of explosive force 33% greater than gasoline vapor under the same consumption conditions. Even though the proposed source (water) is universally available and very cheap – less of it would be needed to power engines traveling the same distances.
3. The improved safety of a car carrying a tank of water for fuel instead of gasoline is also significant.

Technologic advancements working toward fully electric vehicles are laudable and should proceed with all due haste. But for a number of future decades there will still be millions of vehicles

46

around the world polluting the atmosphere with carbon dioxide and other noxious gases from their exhausts. Converting them all to burning hydrogen in their cylinders using water as a carrying medium will eliminate this – while greatly reducing the need for petroleum production, with all its associated problems noted above. The economic advantages of turning water into fuel (whether at personal or national levels) are so obvious as to not need exposition.

America's military should undertake the conversions necessary to accomplish this change for many strategic as well as economic reasons. Fueling is one of the major concerns of operational logistics in any military action. This conversion would reduce those issues to nearly inconsequential levels. Our Navy's surface ships would be completely released from fuel-based tactical constraints and the multi-billion dollar infrastructure issues caused by the need for fuel oil. Commercial ships of all types could also take advantage of the vast electrolytic solution just outside their hulls.

Option 5: Move Our Electricity Underground.

All power lines, residential and industrial, should be put underground – period. Some arguments favoring this proposal are almost silly: "Do high-voltage electric fields overhead disturb the health and well-being of people and animals below?" [Answer: Who knows?] Others are more direct and totally relevant to our future, such as the truly sad and dangerous experiences of having electricity to millions of people disrupted by passing storms that knock down poles and cause trees to fall over power lines. Solar storms, which we will never have any control over, have also been shown to knock out power grids. [1989 in Quebec, for one example.] These concerns, and others in the spectrum between them, can be addressed by the obvious solution: put all electrical transmission lines underground in secure and technologically-advanced conduits. The expense of excavation and pipe-laying will be fully amortized as each new severe storm fails to disrupt vital electrical services.

CHAPTER 9 – Housing Ourselves

The State of Affairs

The most basic human necessities are usually listed as food, shelter, and clothing. How Americans live is uniquely tied to where they live. Nearly every part of America is frequented by disasters of distinct types that routinely cause some people to lose the use of their homes, either temporarily or permanently. Fires occur everywhere, torrential rains cause mudslides, rivers overflow their banks, earthquakes shake down structures without warning, and tornados descend from stormy skies to destroy everything in their paths. When the total number and severity of these disruptions are taken into account, America seems like one of the most dangerous places in the world to live.

Any of these disasters can occur anywhere in the world, but no other country has the number and severity of tornados that rake across the midsection of America every year. North America is the world's only large land mass where warm air from the subtropics can push northward unimpeded by mountain chains to directly clash with colder air from sub-polar regions. The violent collisions of those air masses spawn hundreds of destructive twisters every year.

Every year, too many Americans are forced pick up the pieces of their shattered homes and communities – and try to reassemble the lives they had enjoyed just a few days earlier. No one can stop the storms – indeed, they will be getting worse and more frequent in the decades to come. But we can stop placing ourselves in harm's way rather easily, while also reaping some other benefits. The traditional place to seek protection when tornados strike is someplace underground. An interior room in a frame house provides little protection from nearby twisters and none at all from a direct strike.

Another wasteful practice seen every year when hurricanes approach our coasts is the hasty nailing of plywood sheets over exposed window panes. Residents and business owners anxious to protect expensive picture windows compete with each other to acquire the lumber that will hopefully save their glass. The storm passes and then they contend with storing the now-unnecessary wood somewhere nearby or wastefully discarding it – until the next storm comes along.

Another disheartening sight every year is the combustion of homes and businesses that Americans have placed in areas prone to wildfires. If not already driven by high winds, the firestorms create their own and throw burning cinders on fresh tinder everywhere. Distraught residents lucky enough to escape with their lives will express gratitude for that circumstance while bemoaning the loss of their property.

Option 1: Go Deep.

Americans living and working in tornado-prone regions should build all of their structures – homes, stores, offices, and whatever else, underground. Three feet down will adequately protect any building from the worst tornado. With two mirrors set at 45° angles in a periscope fashion, every window in such a house would have the same view of the outside as if it were sitting atop the property. When severe storms of any type approach, the periscopes could be lowered to avoid damage and then raised later when the danger has passed. This will also offer complete protection from fires of any external origin.

The structures most heavily damaged by severe storms are the modular housing known as "trailers" or mobile homes. Their flimsy construction provides no protection whatever and only feeds the debris danger when their shards are flung about by high winds. They can all be made safe quickly and easily by placing them in trenches where they currently stand. The periscope window technique can provide residents with the same views as if they were above ground. (Actually those views would be improved by removing the sight of their neighbors' double-wides, which are often just beyond an arm's reach.)

In addition to the safety concerns just noted, energy savings for both heating and cooling will be significant enough to justify this type of construction in all areas of the country. Existing examples of how much energy is saved when someone has placed their home underground – particularly when combined with modern construction techniques, is nothing less than truly dramatic. Even in cities we should be building downward, not upward –

wherever the geology will permit. When all power lines are also underground, savings will accrue even faster as power grid disruptions are avoided.

Option 2: Go Strong Where You Can't Go Down.

There are many locations, particularly along America's eastern and southern coasts, where building underground isn't possible or practical – even far from the waters that may rise up to destroy. But that doesn't mean that we have to just keep rebuilding our structures in the same mistaken patterns.

I once worked for an architectural designer who described to me the conditions he encountered for a project on Galveston Island in Texas. The island is basically an ocean-facing sandbar. The first ground solid enough for a building's foundation was about twelve feet below the surface. The local building codes required that all living spaces be at least thirteen feet above sea level. Then the prospects for a hurricane with devastating side-winds are always present. His design solutions were ingenious – and should be copied all along these coasts.

For his project, wood pilings were driven down through the muck until they reached a solid level. Each piling was topped by a steel cap fitted with mountings for trusses that supported the first occupied floors of the building. The living and working areas of each building were designed so that no large flat surface existed on any side of the structure. The windows and sliding glass doors all had built-in panels of wood next to them – to quickly slide into place and lock down when needed. No hurried rush to the lumber yard would be necessary because the window protection was already there. The truss support design made the buildings stronger, not weaker, as the sideways force of the winds grew. And there was the added benefit of shaded parking down between the struts of the trusses during non-stormy times.

Option 3: Don't Ignore the Past.

One thing modern Americans have not done well with respect to housing themselves is to seriously consider the advantages provided by architectural modes already existing in the areas where they have moved. I grew up in Southern California where the challenges to structures are wildfires, mudslides, earthquakes, and seasonal torrential rains. The Spanish / Mexican culture that Americans displaced when they moved in used a style of architecture uniquely appropriate to the region – for a low-density population. There is no doubt that unreinforced mud brick structures like adobe are problematic during earthquakes and have little place in our current urban high-rise world. But the red tile roofs of that style are a definitive benefit during seasons of heat and fire. The modern residential prevalence of wood shake and asphalt shingling on roofs in the area should be curtailed. Many areas of California could benefit from increased use of the soil beneath our feet to create the walls around us and roofs over our heads.

There are many other places in America where we could better integrate those structures we do keep above ground into architectural styles more in keeping with their natural surroundings – as often revealed in their local histories.

Option 4: Don't Pay For It Repeatedly.

While the loss of anyone's property can be a tragedy emotionally affecting us to some degree, providing them with a low-cost government loan or insurance guarantee to rebuild the same structure in the same place is a folly that affects all of us. Those loans or guarantees should be provided only upon the condition that the individual or business rebuild elsewhere or in a manner that can assure the loss will not be repeated. Bottom Line: Do It Once, Not Twice.

No matter how carefully we plan for disasters and how hard we try to avoid them, the unexpected can always occur. America must adopt a basic philosophy of designing structures that will not need replacement because of disasters. In short that means moving back from the waters; digging down not going up; building smarter with respect to all threats; and not repeating the same patterns that fail – even if those failures might be infrequent. Our current constant rebuilding to recover from known hazards is wasteful and simply stupid.

CHAPTER 10 – Commerce

The State of Affairs

Nature operates on the principle of Bounty to provide for the needs of all consumers of whatever species. There are more plankton in the seas than all the little fishes, shrimps, whales, and other filter feeders could ever consume. Huge numbers of these creatures provide the food for a myriad of bigger ones, who in turn are consumed by those still larger. Cows graze in fields of grass growing in sunshine provided in abundance by the star that created the Earth. The biological science of Ecology is replete with examples of how the natural world accommodates both producers and consumers in much the same way that air fills a balloon. Every niche possible is filled by someone or something that interacts with all the world around it.

What we in the western world have long called "Free Enterprise" operates on just that principle to guide what "The Market" provides to consumers. If a desire for something appears to exist, before long someone will arrive on the scene to provide it. It's a natural thing – a wondrous thing. Like a true force of human nature, this process has pervaded most cultures around the world throughout recorded history.

During the 19th century an alternative philosophy – Communism – was proposed. A few small scale experiments were conducted in this country and other places, erroneously citing Native American tribal living as an exemplary reference. Then early in the 20th century a revolution in Russia established a brutal dictatorship that directed all of its nation's economics under that otherwise well-intentioned banner. For 74 years it provided a stark example of how inferior planned economics can be to the natural economics of a "free market" system. They could never engineer into their system the essential principle of Bounty because they didn't believe it was necessary – and probably thought it counterproductive.

But even natural forces are not perfect – and not necessarily the best that America can achieve. Improving on the "free market" will be simple, though many people might regard some of the following ideas as "counter-intuitive".

Option 1: Recognize that Economics Is a Religion, Not a Science.

The terminology of Economics even fits: Do you believe in "Free Enterprise"? Do you know anyone who once believed in "Communism"? If it were a science, repeated application of similar actions under similar circumstances would achieve the same results. That is a hallmark of Science. In Economics, it seldom happens. Economic predictions are proved wrong more often than forecasting weather for a springtime picnic in the Midwest.

As a religion, Economics should not be entitled to "Laws", though "Theorems", "Postulates", and "Assumptions" may still apply. One of its most cherished fallacies is its "Law of Supply and Demand". It should recognized by everyone that the real operating principle is that, under "Free Enterprise", sellers are free to "charge whatever the traffic will bear" at the point of each sale. As the perceived supply of a commodity grows scarce, unregulated producers feel free to charge more money for what they're selling, even though their costs have remained the same. When second-tier intermediaries ("speculators") get involved in the pipeline, things really get twisted. The prices charged start fluctuating not merely on actual supply but also on the expectations of supply, whether current or future – real or perceived. In all of this, at every step, the players are free to charge whatever they think they can get away with asking – regardless of the commodity's true value – current or future.

Option 2: Establish Price Morality In Commerce.

All products and services should be priced at a certain percentage above their production and marketing cost, regardless of demand. This should be established as a basic factor of moral behavior in the marketplace. If I make something that cost $100 to produce and present to the market, I shouldn't feel right about trying to get $200 for it – even if the market demand for it would set a price of $300. The relentless historic drive to maximize profits at the expense of society has brought American (and also most Western) business well past the brink of moral bankruptcy.

Option 3: Establish Earnings Morality.

No one should be allowed to set their own salary. Even nego-
tiated contracts (such as for entertainment and sports stars)
should be factored as multiples of the average wage for the general population. Those multiples should not be allowed to climb to
astronomical levels. Entrepreneurial profits should be heavily
taxed (perhaps to zero) after rising above a defined multiple of the
average wage earner's annual income. Critics who say this will
stifle innovation simply don't know enough about the innate desire
of people to create and share. Most inventions are created
through the excitement of inspiration, not just a desire for profits.

Option 4: Establish Managerial Morality.

Corporate Boards of Directors should be prohibited from own-
ing stock in the companies they manage – or their competitors.
Corporations have become servants of the stock market, directing
most of their actions toward looking good on annual prospectus
sheets – ignoring long-term actions that would be better for their
company and its personnel. This has resulted in the gutting of
corporate employee pension programs (often for the sake of the
directors' "golden parachutes") and the dismantling of meaningful
employee benefits and training programs. A company's workforce
is NOT a dispensable feature of its corporate environment.

Option 5: Establish Morality in Interest Rate Charges.

The Depository Institutions Deregulation and Monetary Control
Act passed by Congress in 1980 strengthened the Federal Reserve's control over all financial institutions in America and permitted credit unions and savings & loans to create checking accounts
for their customers. It also removed all controls over the interest
rates that financial companies could charge for loans and credit
cards. This feature of the act has led to incredible abuses of the
public trust that must be reversed as soon as possible.

Option 6: Reinstitute the Postal Service As a Fully Governmental Entity.

America should not be the only major industrialized-commercialized nation in the world that lacks a national postal service for its citizens. Article One of the Constitution defines the Postal Service as an "...independent establishment of the executive branch of the Government of the United States." The 1970 disarticulation of the Post Office from the rest of the Federal Government should be reversed and its continued operation ensured for the benefit of all Americans. The experience of recent decades has demonstrated that such service to our citizens cannot and should not be operated as a "bottom line for profit" organization. Postage rates shouldn't be held artificially low by subsidizing operating costs with taxes, but the vehicles, permanent property [Post Offices, mail boxes, etc.], and personnel costs are fully in the province of the Government to support.

Currently, the overall volume of mail carried by the Postal Service is declining due to increased reliance on electronic media for business and personal affairs. The reduced revenues received by the Post Office will endanger its survival unless it is once again fully underwritten by the Federal Government as a public service. If, in some future decade or century, the use of paper and paper products is truly eliminated, the Post Office might then be allowed to become a part of history. Until that happens however, preserving the existence of America's postal services is essential.

Option 7: Revolutionize Shipping and Transportation.

A. **Ground:** 1. Reregulate the trucking industry and outlaw long haul trucking.

Since trucking was deregulated in 1980, the number and size of 18-wheel behemoths on the nation's highways has increased significantly. Proponents of the act cite improved supply to consumers, reduced inventories for suppliers, and increased rate competition between carriers as positive benefits of deregulation.

One thing they neglect to cite are the incredibly long hours most truckers put in at the controls of their vehicles. Trucking companies will be the first to say they don't permit their drivers to

55

log more than the number of hours that federal guidelines permit. But it should surprise no one that what's in the log book won't match closely with what's on the highway. Driven to maximize profits for themselves and their bosses, drivers will push themselves to their own perceived limits of endurance. Unfortunately for some – and also other drivers they kill or injure – they quite often push themselves far beyond those limits.

Another aspect not cited is the relaxation of safety standards that always stems from a deregulated environment. Management personnel of trucking companies may know full well that equipment safety is a cost-saving measure, but the urge to accomplish the day's workload easily overpowers the better judgment to inspect and repair vehicles going out on that shift when they themselves are the only ones to police their own behavior. My family and I live in the part of America where Interstate 76 (the Pennsylvania Turnpike which tracks westward over the Appalachians from Philadelphia through Pittsburgh) intersects with Interstate 81 (running southward from New York state to Knoxville, Tennessee). In our neighborhood 18-wheelers outnumber cars on the interstates by a significant factor every day of the year. Local news reports frequently report fatal crashes involving trucks that generally involve either driver error or equipment failure. This must be changed.

The other cost embedded in deregulation that is rarely considered is the increased stress on the pavement of the interstate highway system. Each legally-loaded truck puts 7,000 times the wear on highway pavement as a car does. The many illegally-loaded trucks on the roads stress the pavement as if they were each 14,000 cars. The repair and replacement costs for the nation's highways and bridges are made much higher by the constant truck traffic they currently bear.

But a better alternative is (and always has been) already available: Railroads carry freight at a ton-mile cost only 10% as high as truck traffic. Almost all long-haul freight shipments should be made by rail, not highway, for this and the other reasons noted above. A somewhat greater investment in nationwide inventories might be necessary because of the additional handling required at new depot points where freight would be removed from the rails and shifted to short-haul trucks, but this would be more than offset by the improved useful life of the country's interstate highway system.

The necessary reregulation would then apply to short-haul trucking to ensure proper drayage rates and maintain local highway safety. An additional human benefit is that truckers could once again become family men instead of the highwaymen they are now. Because of the way household goods are handled commercially, moving van companies might be made exempt from this option.

    2.   <u>Shorten the trailers</u>. All trucking trailers should be brought back to their historic non-leviathan length of 40 feet. The nation's existing fleets of 53 foot trailers should be phased out and their materials recycled. They are a menace everywhere they go. If long-haul trucking does continue, all trailers must be shortened and tandem trailers should also be outlawed.

B. Sea: <u>Make overseas shipments underwater</u>. America should establish a new fleet of freight vessels that travel as shallow-depth submarines. Not subject to the whims of the weather, these ships could reach foreign ports in safety at any time of the year. They should also be flagged in American ports if they're owned by Americans. Technologic advancements in materials, electronics, and other scientific fields can be used to re-establish America's pre-eminence in cargo transportation – and as many other commercial areas as possible.

C. Air:

    1.   <u>Reregulate the air travel and air cargo industries</u>. Since the Federal government deregulation several decades ago, harsh competition has caused serious erosion of the provider bases for the air travel and air cargo industries. While deregulation seems a fine idea in theory, in practice it creates an environment where cutting costs becomes a paramount concern – usually at the expense of service, schedule, and safety. Since so many citizens now rely on air travel as a regular means of transportation, passenger fares should be reregulated as a public utility. Routes should be regulated to balance the business between competing providers. Safety procedures and equipment maintenance sched-

ules must be reinforced immediately. Currently the crew in an aircraft's cockpit is the first line of defense against equipment failures in flight – when they should be the last.

2.   Extend the hours when flights are scheduled. Establish 24-hour operating schedules at airports where it is necessary to reduce air and ground traffic congestion.

3.   Give them more wings. Aircraft designers should experiment with multiple-winged commercial craft. Two or three sets of lifting wings mean the wings could be shorter, enabling more planes to fit into current airport docking areas.

4.   Replace the control technology. Fly-by-wire electric motor technology should replace hydraulic systems in all planes. A single-point failure of a hydraulic system can spell disaster for an airborne vehicle, which would not be true for an array of electric motors performing the same functions.

D.   Air on the Ground: Develop a new method of air travel – through tubes on or under the ground. The air tube technology used in the "mail chutes" at bank drive-up windows should be expanded into a cargo and passenger service industry. The front end of the vehicles would be shaped like the heads of blue whales – funneling air from in front down underneath the body. The vehicles would use wheels only in stations and while accelerating to and decelerating from their "flight speed". As more air is pumped out of the tubes, higher and higher velocities would be possible – very likely exceeding the speeds currently attained by free-flying aircraft. Some operational advantages:

1.   No onboard fuel. Passenger cabins and freight cars would be moved forward by the force of electromagnets in the bottom of the tubes, pulling on steel plates on the undersides of the vehicles. The vehicles would carry no fuel or batteries – except minor ones which might be needed in emergencies. Horizontal loops of copper wire around the steel plates would have a current induced in them by virtue of being pulled through the magnetic field in the tubes. This would provide all the electrical power needed by the car except when in a station, where inductive connections can be easily provided.

2.   More doors. Each passenger car would have at least three entrances – on the lower half of the vehicle. All passengers

would stow their own baggage in racks at the entrances. Attendants would help lift bags when required – and would secure all luggage with tagged identification. Passengers would not be allowed to access their baggage after the vehicle has started in motion.

      3.   <u>More passenger freedom</u>. No seat belts would be required and every seat would have access to an aisle. Beverages and snacks would be available at a counter near the center of the car. There would be none of the usual "services" airlines perform currently, now done mostly just to keep passengers entertained in their seats.

      4.   <u>Safe travel ways</u>. The tube tracks would be supported under tripods mounted along existing interstate highways or railroad rights-of-way. For protection from earthquakes, supporting cables would be looped around the tubes and anchored to the tripods with springs at their ends. In tornado-prone areas, the tripod-tube assemblies should ideally be mounted in underground tunnels or in trenches sufficiently deep to provide lateral protection from high winds.

Experimentation with this new transportation mode could begin with retail-level freight-forwarders like UPS and FedEx working in a federally-sponsored consortium that would, in effect, create a "package pipeline" for high-speed and ecologically-sound delivery between designated processing points. With full deployment of this technique, those transporters could eliminate their current fleets of aircraft and large-trucks.

    E. **Automobiles:**   Replace the glass windshields of cars and trucks with wide-screen electronic displays of the upcoming environment. The area could be padded internally for driver and passenger safety while eliminating the danger / expense of broken glass from the strikes of road debris. At night the visual displays could use infra-red wavelengths to fully reveal wildlife and humans currently hidden from view. Headlamp wattages could be reduced to small warning lamps for oncoming vehicles. Small cameras could replace the vehicles' side mirrors, with wider-angled displays on the corners of the viewing area.

CHAPTER 11 – Politics, National

The State of Affairs

One of the sadder things to observe in American political life is to see what happens to a good idea on its way to becoming law. As soon as a Congressional bill lands in the hopper and is published in the Record, lobbyists start circling over it like vultures above a carcass in the desert. The modern term for these vermin is "special interest groups", but the effect is the same now as it always has been – to twist and distort any government action to favor their supporters. Some of them even collaborate amongst themselves to exercise influence over bills that don't affect their paying constituents directly, but might affect the clients of some of their partners in crime.

Option 1:   Eliminate Lobbyists – NOW!!

All professional lobbyists must be driven from the halls of government at every level. By law, if possible, by brute force if necessary. Government personnel, whether elected or appointed, who deal with them should be prosecuted together with them. Members of Congress in both houses claim to carefully listen to their constituents' mail, email, and phone call messages. Other than glad-handing voters at political rallies, those should be the only outside contacts considered legitimate for any elected official.

Option 2:   Improve the Presidential Primary Process.

America's current process for selecting Presidential candidates through a primary election system allows ideologues to take over their political parties too easily. Single-issue groups gain sway in their parties that is out-sized in proportion to their actual numbers within the party. While their enthusiasm may be admirable, their narrow focus is not generally in the best interests of either party. Even front-running contenders sometimes find themselves supporting rather untenable positions just to garner support among these fanatics early in the race – and then try rather comically to backpedal during the general election campaign. This can be improved by instituting <u>one national "primary" election day</u>. This proposal would effectively reduce the outsized influence exercised on political parties by own their ideological "wings". It should be adopted as soon as possible.

Option 3:   Shorten the Presidential Selection Process.

For a number of decades now, American citizens have been subjected to the spectacle of politicians beginning their runs for the Presidency shortly after the office has been filled for the current term. With the suggested one six-year term for presidents in place the incumbent, at least, will be excused from further posturing. It will probably take a combined effort of several elements of American society to dissuade hopeful politicians from prematurely assaulting the rest of us with their own career ambitions. Formation of "exploratory committees" and similar activities should be strongly discouraged (or simply not allowed) until six months before the one national primary day. Formal announcements of someone's candidacy should not be taken seriously by anyone until that date as well.

Option 4:   Abolish Political Action Committees, PERIOD!

PACs have no reason to exist other than to unduly influence the opinions of Americans regarding the topic of each PAC's particular interest. While nominally protected by the Constitutional guarantee of Freedom of Speech, the nature of their actions inhibits the speech freedom of other citizens. Someone with a megaphone doesn't have a greater right to free speech than anyone else. The contributors to PACs have every right to speak as loudly as they want – as **individuals who** are free to **identify themselves** when they speak. A group or a corporation is NOT a person. The cloak of secrecy inherent in these organizations eliminates their right to free expression on political – or other matters. These groups are simply advertisers – and should be treated as such. When any PAC interacts with incumbent government personnel it should be regarded as a lobbying transaction – subject to the penalties noted just above.

CHAPTER 12 – Politics, International

The State of Affairs

In future centuries and millennia, should mankind survive, America will be known as history's best example of what can be achieved when citizens are able to cooperate freely in forming the society in which they live and work. America has evolved significantly since the days when European thinkers regarded us as an intellectual curiosity. As noted in the Forward above, the liberal application of liberty and individual freedom applied to our society nurtured its democratic urges to the point where we have long regarded them as institutions and inalienable rights. The rest of the world either already emulates, or would like to emulate, many of our traditions and copy our success.

But there are still dangerous places in the world where American interests are challenged severely and frequently. In several unfortunate circumstances recently America's military might has been used to bludgeon two unruly dictatorships to death and assist the international community in the destruction of a third. As laudable – even justifiable – as our aims might have been, under international law and the view of History the actions were illegal.

Option 1:   Lead By Example, Not By Force.

Generally speaking, Americans are happy to wish emerging nations well in their endeavors to emulate us. But we need to understand that we must lead by example in this, not by force of arms. Our story during the first decade of this century has been marred by two situations where the American government tried to create democratic institutions in countries that never had them before by demolishing their existing societies. At this writing those experiments are still in progress. Time will tell if the efforts have been successful or whether, like growing vegetables in a hydroponic garden, the fruits of our labors will wither when the gardener comes back to his regular fields at home. In short, we can't create democracies down the barrel of a gun. Not all societies are mature enough to establish stable democratically-elected governments. Americans need to realize that and be prepared to live in a world that may at times be less than truly civilized, to our tastes at least.

Option 2:   Bring the Troops Home Entirely.

More than three generations after the end of World War II, America still has troops permanently stationed on the soil of its opponents. This may have made sense when those societies were still trying to rebuild from the devastation wreaked upon them by the war – to forestall the re-emergence of dictators from among a possibly dissatisfied populace. But that time passed long ago. Shooting in the Korean War ended six decades ago and America still has thousands of troops stationed near where the truce lines were drawn. This situation is somewhat more justified because of the continued existence of a ruthless dictatorship nearby. Whether the people we were defending in that conflict are now fully able to defend their own government from destruction is an issue of on-going concern.

The underlying reason these deployments still exist is that the American Department of Defense has a long-standing strategic policy of maintaining a military foothold in areas that may at some future point require a resurgence of force. (A lesson learned during World War II from having to mount the D-Day invasion of Normandy from across the English Channel.) America also maintains "forward basing" in prospective problem areas around the world. [Bahrain and Djibouti are current examples.]

These understandable concerns of the Defense Department are now obsolete because of its own prowess in technology and logistics. The advent of accurately guided sea-borne and air-launched cruise missiles has significantly changed the battlefield – no matter where that battlefield might be, except perhaps central Asia. Advanced placement of tactical supplies can be accomplished with our Navy's "sea basing" concept, which would build on the maritime prepositioning squadrons already floating in several strategic but little-noticed oceanic locations. Our fighting ships no longer need to pull into ports in semi-friendly forward countries to quickly and effectively accomplish their missions. In short, we do not need to keep permanently stationed troops in foreign countries.

Modern piracy is a continuing concern that only a few navies of the world can address. We should not lose focus on those problem areas. While the just-noted bases in Bahrain and Djibouti are reasonably well-placed to deal with the currently-active pirates coming out of Somalia, a forward sea-base effort near the shipping lanes off the Horn of Africa would be more productive. Pirates in the Malacca Straight area of Indonesia could be effectively thwarted by a well-placed group of ships working offshore near Singapore.

Option 3:   Move the United Nations Headquarters.

United Nations Headquarters should be moved out of New York City and placed in the Gaza Strip, sitting in between Israel and Egypt. New York can use the real estate and Gaza desperately needs some economic basis for a national government and culture. Currently 1.6 million people subsist there on UN relief supplies. [1 million of them are Palestinians whose forebears were forcibly displaced and moved there as refugees in 1948 when Israel was created by a UN mandate. They have had little to do for the last six decades other than hope for the destruction of those whom they view as their oppressors.] There is an unemployment rate of 40%, ranking them 183rd out of the world's 199 countries. 70% of the population subsists below the UN guidelines for poverty. Deadly strife is constant because the renegade Palestinian group calling itself the Islamic Resistance Movement (HAMAS) refuses to acknowledge Israel's right to exist and also argues, sometimes violently, with the Palestinian Authority in the West Bank while claiming to administer the government of Gaza.

All of these injustices could be relieved by an international imposition of order justified by relocation of the United Nations Headquarters. A set of new structures built on unoccupied seaside property surrounded by a new international airport on the landward side would firmly establish an unassailable foothold of sanity in the Strip. From there UN troops could advance through the four populated areas and scour out all offensive weapons from the populace. HAMAS would have to be disbanded and any of its participants unwilling to concede should be incarcerated until they agree.

Israel would be instructed to fully withdraw to its pre-1967 borders and the UN would be able to more closely monitor and provide international protection to all parties. The Israeli settlements that have been built in the territory should be vacated as-is and turned over to Palestinians.

This concept could be extended to include the entire Sinai Peninsula – providing UN military and peacekeeping forces a permanent operations base and training area close to those geographic regions where they are mostly likely to be needed.

The Golan Heights of Syria should be ceded to the UN as an observation post in that region.

Option 4:   End Slavery.

A few years ago National Geographic magazine devoted an issue to modern slavery. In its forward, the editor noted that there are more slaves in the world today than there ever were in history. I put the issue reverently on my bookshelf and did not read any further. In the many years I've subscribed, it is the only issue I've never read from cover to cover. As Americans we must do whatever we can economically, politically, or militarily to end heinous trafficking in human beings. Many of the products Americans consume – food and clothing included – are produced and transported by forced, unpaid, captive laborers. We must uncover and punish both the primary participants and their hidden conspirators – governmental and otherwise – who perpetuate this foul dehumanizing practice.

Option 5:   Continue Nuclear Disarmament.

Strictly speaking, this is not really an option. It must be done to ensure the continued survival of mankind as we know it. Nuclear weapons have only two conceivable purposes:

1) Ensure the destruction of a particular target that must be achieved, regardless of cost and;
2) Raise the specter of a fiery death in the minds and hearts of your enemies, demoralizing them to point of surrender.

But nuclear weapons have serious well known drawbacks, in addition to their incredible expense. Cruise missiles made them militarily obsolete through targeting precision. [The first reason.] The end of the Cold War made them politically obsolete on the "global stage" of the old super-powers. [The second reason.]

When America and Russia finally get down to the levels of weapons that other countries have, those other players should be included in the discussions as equals and the reductions should continue. United Nations inspections of all former national stockpiles must be instituted world-wide. Any country discovered to have newly-acquired nuclear weapons technology must be closely monitored to ensure they dismantle their processes. Otherwise joint international (or possibly UN) efforts to destroy all of their production facilities should begin. Conventional forces that America, Russia, and other allies could bring to bear against any renegade nation will be more than sufficient to ensure that destruction.

CHAPTER 13 – Religion

The State of Affairs

While not a widely-known fact these days, it is acknowledged by historians that a significant fraction of America's Founding Fathers were Deists. They believed in God, but were hesitant to describe their thoughts about how God proceeded to run the Universe after creating it. Having observed the troubles caused in the Old World when governments meddled in the religious beliefs of their citizens, they very wisely declared in the first Amendment to the Constitution that the federal government would not promote or hinder the establishment or management of religions in America. Later on, passage of the Fourteenth Amendment struck down any state or local government's ability to do so. As a result of these fully correct and proper actions, Americans have been free to worship as they choose, provided that the exercise of their beliefs don't violate public laws or endanger other people.

Option 1:   Maintain the Public Commitment to Separation of Church and State.

Recent historical events (Iran since 1979 and America under George W. Bush) have demonstrated that theocracies don't work – and never will. This country's tradition of establishing a respectful distance between government and institutions of faith must be bolstered firmly – and never allowed to falter. The Bush-era "faith-based initiatives" were inherently unconstitutional and should have been denounced as such immediately upon their initial proposal. Future efforts to re-institute such travesties must be quickly trounced.

Option 2:   Eliminate Tax Exemptions for Religious Organizations.

Charitable organizations should be exempt from taxation because of the good works they perform for American society as a whole. But those portions of the income derived for, and property held by, any organization that are not directly devoted to charitable works should be taxed. In short, if the proceeds from the collection plate passed around next Sunday are not devoted to documented charitable efforts before the end of the year, they should be taxed. Donations made to churches that merely increase their buildings' grandeur or opulent furnishings should be taxed. Fixing the roof is fine – gilding the alter is not.

Option 3:   Reformulate Islam.

Internationally, America must insist to Muslim countries that – if they intend their religion to be fully accepted in the modern world, they must get their religious leaders to contritely renounce violence – in any degree – as an acceptable expression of faith. While some of the most holy imams refuse to scratch fleas because of the harm that might do to some of God's creatures, other mullahs incite their faithful to the worst kinds of violence against men, women, and children – citing verses in Koran that encourage action against any and all "non-believers". In 2008 a highly-respected Muslim seminary in northern India called the Ulama Deoband announced that from its review of Koranic religious law, followers of Islam should realize that violence against all other well-meaning and innocent human beings is sinful. This fatwa must be more widely broadcast across the world and its basic message repeated by other Muslim schools. In all countries, Muslim organizations not associated with governments must take up the challenge as well. It won't be easy turning back the currently widespread tradition of violent religious decrees, but it is VERY necessary for the future wellbeing of mankind.

Option 4:   Encourage Gift-giving During Mawlid – the Islamic "Christmas".

The gratuitous giving of gifts to family, friends, and acquaintances in late December each year is one of the principle economic driving forces in the Christian world. When the practice is descried by would-be aesthetics as a debasement of the Faith, they ignore the tremendous economic effect it has on economies at local, state, national, and international levels. The relative economic difference between the Christian and non-Christian worlds, while changing somewhat now, is still very stark. Worldwide European colonial domination for several centuries and Christmas gift-giving are the two primary reasons. While little can be done internationally to redress the sins of the past, we can improve prospects for mankind's future by extending practices that are known to be economically beneficial.

Mawlid an-Nabi (Birth of the Prophet) is already observed in much of the Islamic world. The lunar calendar used to identify the annual date changes by 11-12 days each year in terms of the Gregorian calendar that European cultures use, but causes no problem for the Islamic faithful to determine the date.

What America should do is actively encourage Muslims to begin the same gratuitous gift-giving frenzy so prevalent in the Christian world. This will be an uphill road with a slope somewhat steeper than the establishment of Europeans' Xmas had to climb. But it should be recognized by all as a vitally-necessary component of the economics of healthy societies. Religion actually has little to do with it.

CHAPTER 14 – UNIVERSAL MEDICIAL CARE

The State of Affairs

A burning issue of critical importance to America's place in the modern world is the medical care provided to our citizens and the burgeoning, almost explosive, costs of that care – particularly as they crossover from their working livelihoods into retirement. In November 1945 President Truman proposed creating a nation-wide health plan which would have effectively provided hospital and doctors' care to all areas of the country, both urban and rural. Because he proposed a tax-funded national health insurance plan it was denounced as "socialized medicine" by the AMA and roundly defeated in Congress shortly thereafter. [See Chapter 11, Option 1 for comments on lobbyists.] The same arguments were raised less successfully twenty years later when Medicare was passed for Social Security recipients and President Johnson appropriately gave Harry Truman credit while signing the bill into law.

America is approaching a crisis of funding for both medical care and retirement that has many people justifiably alarmed. Fewer workers are entering the workforce and more are retiring from it. Those retirees are living longer and requiring more medical care for longer periods. Many very expensive technological advances in medicine are being deployed for humanitarian treatment of seniors – even when they and their families can't afford to pay for them. America seems to be driving a fast car down a short blind alley with a big brick wall at the end of it.

A big part of the problem is the paradigm under which the discussions are being held: Tying medical care to insurance and then tying insurance to employment simply hasn't worked – and never will. It moves vast amounts of money into the financial system (in the form of insurance company profits) and away from the medical community where it belongs. The arguments are heated and associated data quoted to bolster the many viewpoints create a bewildering constellation of factoids. The bottom line is that something sweeping must be done – but what? Some ideas:

Option 1:   Really "Socialize" Our Medicine.

The government could just draft doctors, nurses, and medical technicians into federal service while taking over the hospitals, labs, and drug companies they work with. Or the government could mandate that services be provided, with all carefully-audited expenses paid from taxes. While an upheaval of this kind might seem really scary to many people, it would significantly reduce the overall amounts of money required to provide medical services to all Americans.

Option 2:   Leave the Doctors and Hospitals Alone But Publicly Fund the Insurance.

The Canadian model, often called a "single payer" system, has been in place since 1986 and more than 85% of that country's citizens express thorough satisfaction with the results. America currently devotes nearly 16% of its Gross Domestic Product (GDP) to medical costs – the highest percentage of any industrialized nation. We get less service for it than any of the rest and many millions of our citizens are still without medical insurance (and therefore services) of any kind, except the most expensive service – trips to the local emergency room (which they also can't pay for afterwards).

Option 3:   Reform the malpractice industry.

There once was a time in America when doctors were strongly discouraged from testifying against each other in court. While that effectively restrained the costs of malpractice insurance – and thereby overall medical costs, the situation was patently unfair to patients. But for several decades now the opposite situation has prevailed and reflexively the medical community has tried to minimize its risk by maximizing diagnostic expenditures – which the entire nation is forced to amortize through higher insurance premiums.

Canons of medical treatment for specific problems are well known and taught to doctors as a routine part of their training. The American legal system must be made to establish a canon of its

71

own – to leave medical personnel unmolested, regardless of patients' real or imagined claims – when the established rules of medicine have been applied to the particular case. While every American does have the right to express any grievance in court, the nation's judges and juries should routinely and uniformly deny malpractice claims that don't show medical merit – as defined in those established standards.

Option 4: Eliminate Retirement.

When I graduated from high school in the mid-1960s the average life span for men was 72 years and the retirement age was firmly set at 65. While in college I decided that rather than working hard for 40-some years and then retiring for seven years of decrepitude, I would retire first while I was still happily healthy – and then get a job I liked where I wouldn't be subjected to a forced retirement due to age. I spent ten years getting a four-year degree – with several of those years completely "on the loose" and I thoroughly enjoyed my retirement.

In 1975 I started working for the US Army (later on for the US Navy) as a civilian and have significantly contributed, I feel, to my country's national defense. I still do and will continue to do so. During my 40-some years of Federal service I've called my scheme the "pine box" retirement plan. In years of observing coworkers and others, my early view that retirement is an unhealthy thing to do has been confirmed to my own satisfaction.

It should be recognized generally that retirement is detrimental to Americans' health, both physical and mental. Americans define themselves by what they do – just watch the personal introductions on any TV game show. With people living longer, it has become too expensive for society to maintain the existing retirement system. People who can no longer handle the physical demands of their old jobs should be retrained for future careers – without respect to their age. It is only when people can REALLY no longer work at any meaningful job, they should be "retired" under Social Security and Medicare, which should then provide funding for ALL their necessary services without further cost to them.

CHAPTER 15 – GENDER EQUALITY

The State of Affairs

Throughout history one of the saddest and most unfair circumstances of human existence is the treatment of women and girls by the male-dominated societies in which they have been obliged by fate to live. In America (and many of its European forebears) this undeserved inequality ranges through degrees as subtle as male-oriented medical studies that don't adequately consider the effects of diseases and treatments on feminine patients – down through societal tolerance of domestic violence and sexual abuse.

Somewhere between these extremes lie many other travesties such as reduced pay for women who perform work equal or superior to their male co-workers. Objectification of women has always been so pervasive in western culture that women themselves succumb to judging each other on appearance over achievement. Youth and beauty are praised while experience and accomplishment are slighted.

As gently inhumane as these situations may be, the inhumanity suffered by women in Africa and Asia is truly horrific. Dozens of those societies prohibit, suppress, or restrain the basic right of women to a functional education. Many of them also practice and espouse genital mutilation of girls as an "insurance policy" for their future overlords against the prospect of extra-marital attractions. Then finally, in some rural areas of Asia there are places where poor little feminine infants have been simply discarded, left to die in the elements – if not just murdered outright by their parents. A tear comes to my eye and a tear rips through my heart to think of the incredible atrocities committed by nearly all societies through history against the most gentle of those among them.

It is obvious that issues of gender inequity continue to exist worldwide, dividing all societies into splintering groups of human beings – who often don't even realize how pervasive and deep the inequality has extended. This must be reversed for at least two vitally important reasons:

1. <u>Basic fairness and humanity</u>. Nearly every creation story on Earth stresses the differences between man and woman while

endeavoring to minimize the similarities. Those arbitrary distinctions continue through today in every society – directly measureable by the degree to which they are driven by religious orthodox tendencies. While facetiously pretending to "cherish" their women and celebrating the uniqueness they bring to a man's life, the real intent is to "own" the other person – whether with the golden chains of love or the iron fetters of legal and economic domination. When men struggle against each other over a woman it is the prospect of ownership – not emotional attachment – that is the real issue of contention.

On those rare occasions when a woman may be offered a choice between two such aggressors – her best option is usually to choose the one who would do her the least harm. A poor woman making the wrong choice – for whatever reason – can be placing herself at great risk. Even the right choice in that situation can still lead to an unfairness of circumstance and years of complacency – laced with frustration. (Does the princess ever really achieve her "happily ever after" when her choices were dictated by others and not chosen for herself?)

2. Sustaining the human race on Earth. For the last two centuries a debate has raged in academic circles regarding how human beings will sustain themselves on Earth when the population expands past the planet's limited resource capacity. At the end of 2017, there were 7.6 billion human beings in the world. It is estimated that by 2100 that number could increase to 11.8 billion. Robert Malthus, who basically started the debate, maintained in 1798 that improved resource development results in population increases rather than better living conditions. He said that later when degrees of human misery rise sufficiently, population increases eventually level off.

This description of his view is well-known and has been largely been borne out by history during the intervening centuries. But this is not inevitable and its simplistic view of human behavior ignores a great issue of our time. The societies where the birth rates, death rates, and levels of human misery are highest are those that most fiercely oppress women.

A better way has been shown to us by the country of Brazil. In one generation Brazil reduced its per-woman birth rate from

6.7 to 2.1 children by integrating women into its urban work-forces and educational institutions. The United Nations Human Development Index for Brazil rose from 0.59 in 1990 to 0.754 in 2016. (An improvement of 27.8%.) Most assuredly, Brazil has a good deal of improvement yet to make regarding improving the lives of all its citizens, but the point here is that what it has done so far shows what must be done to prevent disastrous worldwide overpopulation. The education and full integration of women into all societies – accompanied by fairness in all areas of life – must be accomplished everywhere. It is imperative for human survival on the planet.

Now to the specifics of what America must do. As noted just above, America treats its feminine citizens much better than many other parts of the world. But it is surely not the best among nations – and all countries need to improve in order to attain true gender equality for all their people.

I have worked for the US Defense Department for 43 years. While I'm sure there have probably been instances of gender abuse within the organization during that time, I have personally never seen or heard of any systemic unequal treatment based on gender. Our pay grades are established by Public Law and are not discriminatory on any visible basis. Promotions are supposed to be based exclusively on merit, can be subjected to external audit, and possibly be challenged legally if suspected to be made otherwise. Ideally, all American businesses should follow the gender-neutral example of the Federal Government in hiring, firing, promotions, and pay.

OPTION 1: Re-establish Efforts towards an Equal Rights Amendment to the US Constitution

Back in 1979, a small number of indifferent state legislatures allowed the Equal Rights Amendment to the US Constitution to expire before it could be fully ratified and made part of our legal landscape. This must be corrected. The Amendment should be resurrected – this time improved to cover the rights of people who chose to change their birth gender or to simply be known as non-gendered. It should then be proposed once again and passed by

Congress. The gender-equality climate of America has greatly evolved during the last 39 years. During the 1970s attempt, 34 of the necessary 38 states ratified the Amendment within the first three years of the seven that were called for. In America's current political and cultural environment, all fifty states should be able to pass ratification acts within the first year. Under the intense public scrutiny that would focus on this issue, I doubt that any state assembly would dare risk the political retribution that would swiftly befall any legislator voting against it.

OPTION 2: Firmly Establish Equal Gender Rights on the State Level

Any American state legislature that has not already accomplished this simple feat should immediately be taken to task for such a reprehensible dereliction of its duty. There can be no excuse for invalidating the worth of feminine participants in any of America's many societies.

OPTION 3: Establish Equal Pay and Rights on Local Levels

Many municipal and county governments across the country have already exercised their right and duty to ensure that all workers in their jurisdictions receive pay commensurate with duties performed – without regard to the gender of their workers.
The Tenth Amendment to the US Constitution says:

"The powers not delegated to the United States by the Constitution, nor prohibited by it to the States, are reserved to the States respectively, or to the people."

Local governments should immediately express their rights here to extend full gender protection to all citizens in employment as well as legal rights. No commercial entity or industry should be permitted to discriminate against anyone on the basis of gender or gender-identity. Local governments do not have to wait for national- or state-level approval to accomplish this.

CHAPTER 16 – Sports

The State of Affairs

One of the most common factors of human life is that as soon as people have a little free time on their hands they engage in recreational sports. While some of those pursuits in primitive cultures may emulate more serious aspects of life like hunting or warfare, almost all peoples at all times have found games to play – with whatever is at hand. Those that can't or don't want to participate are quite often very happy to watch those that do. As societies developed into more complex structures the games played in them followed suit and eventually some high-performing individuals were able to make their livings by becoming professional athletes.

In modern America we have reached an extreme point where exceptional performance in one of the big-money sports (football, baseball, basketball, tennis, or golf) is regarded as an achievement of almost celestial status. The amount of money made by these individuals is quite often also "astronomical". [See Chapter 9, Option 3 for comments on sports salaries.] This causes several situations in America that should be corrected. Many thousands, perhaps millions, of young men and women entertain dreams of "making it big" in the sport of their choice even though only a few hundred of them will ever be able to do so. Many of them forego earnestly preparing for careers that would be more rewarding for their long-term living prospects. The money paid to those who do successfully achieve high professional status is so great that the owners of the teams they join feel forced to charge very high ticket prices to the spectators who want to watch the games being played.

Option 1: Reduce Sports Salaries to Standard Multiples of the Average American Income.

In the early 1950s, Mickey Mantle was the first sports figure to ever be paid more for a year's effort than the American President made that same year. At that point in time and earlier, the average professional baseball player earned a salary about seven times greater than the average American wage earner. Given that their professional careers are a good deal shorter than the average worker, a factor of seven seems reasonable. Other sports where the average career is even shorter than that might have a higher factor imposed and those sports where careers are longer could be constrained by a lower factor.

Financial savings to the teams should be passed to the fans in the form of lower ticket prices. In league sports like baseball and football, this would allow expansion into smaller markets and more fully democratize the sports. That, in turn, would provide more opportunities for players who retire to find coaching or staffing jobs – further reducing a need for overly-high salaries.

The salaries paid to the players could then be augmented by well-defined bonuses for performance achievements. [Highest batting average on the team, conference, or league would gain the player a year-end bonus or specified salary increase for the next year, and so forth. Quarterbacks achieving better performance ratings could be paid higher salaries the next year on that numeric basis.] With this kind of compensatory standardization, players would then be much more likely to settle down with the teams of their choice and once more become the local heroes they used to be, rather than the too-mobile self-interested personal corporations they have become.

Option 2: Build the Stadiums Where the Fans Are.

All stadiums and arenas should be built as close as possible to the population centers they intend to serve. This would reduce driving distances for fans and enable many of them to use public transportation to get to games. The old model provided by New York City's baseball teams (and recently emulated by the San Francisco Giants) should be the norm across the country.

Option 3: Establish Full Gender Equality in All Sports.

Even though the Equal Rights Amendment for women was defeated a few decades ago, America hasn't abandoned the fundamental principle of equality, which is a good thing. What is not a good thing is that the salaries paid for, and fans attracted by,

78

women's versions of our major professional sports lag severely behind that of the men's versions. Professional sports could significantly advance the proposition of gender equality by adopting the playing model of Roller Derby – having men and women compete against members of their own gender in separate sections of all games.

A. Baseball: Women could play the even-numbered innings while men start off the games (and probably finish them) playing in the odd-numbered innings.

B. Football: Women could start the games, playing the odd-numbered periods (which might be increased to six, overall) while men finished off the games in the even numbered periods. This would allow longer resting times for all players to more thoroughly recuperate before resuming their contests and also eliminate the need for "half-time" antics.

C. Basketball, Hockey, Soccer: The football comments apply.

D. Tennis: Gender equality in performing coverage has been established historically. Equality in earnings must also be assured.

E. Golf: Both Professional Golfers' Associations should be combined and play on the same courses at the same times. Women's teeing off locations are already established on all courses to compensate for the greater arm strength of men. There is no reason why women cannot compete in the same tournaments. There is no reason why competing foursomes couldn't be "mixed" like bowling league teams.

Option 4: Eliminate "Sudden Death" Play in Football.

In professional football a coin toss is used to determine which team will first get the ball for the extra time after regulation play. In years past a correct guess of "heads or tails" successfully predicted the game's winner 85% of the time.

A. To reduce the risk of injury to players who are already tired and thus more prone to getting hurt, the coin toss could be used to decide the winner without any further play.

B. A more satisfying and fair alternative would be to play an entire extra playing period. The stronger team will prevail at some point in time – which will be more fairly determined by playing a full period. Football's recent rule change to mandate at least one possession by each team during overtime is a step in the right direction, but a full period would be better.

Option 5: Modernize Football Helmets.

The historic and current structure of face masks on NFL helmets should be replaced by complete face shields of clear hardened plastic. The danger of spinal cord injury to players suffering "face mask" pulls is too great and must be reduced. The solution is obvious and should be adopted immediately. Air holes too small for fingers to fit through could be made in the lower portions of the mask to facilitate breathing. The current "grill work" must be replaced.

Another alternative would be to remove the facemask structures altogether. There are already a number of NFL rules in place regarding "hands to the face" that can protect players as much as the rubber-coated steel now being used.

Option 6: In Baseball, Eliminate the American League's "Designated" Hitters.

Eliminate the "designated hitter" rule in the American League and have pitchers stand at the plate for their normal rounds of batting and base running. Keeping baseball's original playing tactics hasn't hurt team or player performance in the National League, and it is also demonstrated by American League teams during inter-league games and the World Series.

Option 7: Fully Separate Amateur Athletics from Professional Sports.

A. <u>Olympic sports</u>. America's basketball "Dream Team" in the 1992 Barcelona Olympics was a primary example of misapplying the sporting principle. Taking a professional all-star team of over-sized, over-skilled players on the road to see how badly they could trounce every other assemblage of players on the planet was a travesty that should not be repeated. The original vision of the Olympic Games as an amateur competition between citizens of the world should be reinforced, not undermined through the exercise of political or economic leverage. The International Basketball Federation's 1989 decision to allow American NBA players to compete in the Olympics was misguided and should be reversed – while also excluding all other nations' professional players from future Olympics. That ban should also be expanded to all other Olympic sports where athletics can eventually achieve a professional status.

B. <u>College sports</u>. They should be ended. Too many colleges depend on performance of their sports teams for alumni support when everyone should be focused on what institutions of higher learning are supposed to provide to the country. Many young men and women who should be guiding their lives toward useful life-long pursuits are bending their efforts to suit the aims of individuals (both inside and outside the academic institutions) trying to profit from muscular and neurologic skills that will fade with the passage of a few short years. Seats in college classrooms should be reserved for those who will use their academic education as intended, not as a stepping stone to a professional athletic career. The benefits of physical exercise for students can be fully realized through intra-mural sports, and working out in the gymnasiums and outdoor fields of the institutions.

C. <u>End the drafts</u>. The NFL and NBA should adopt professional baseball's "training camp" and "farm system" approach for development of their players. With college sports terminated, individual players interested in pursuing athletic careers could apply directly to the teams of their choice. Prospective players who aren't going to "make it" professionally would find that out early enough in life to earnestly start academic studies in college – or find another trade outside of school. Professional teams would benefit through elimination of the outrageous signing bonuses that result from competing for a few star players in each sport that may have been first identified when they were back in high school – or even earlier.

In Summary

The State of Affairs

Historically and currently, America is the greatest nation on Earth – of that there can be no doubt. Our success has not been achieved without tribulation and risk. The dangers in the world at America's inception have changed, but not diminished. We must always be ready to defend our country with both sacrifice and love. Teddy Roosevelt was right: America will be the land of the free only so long as it is the home of the brave. Most fortunately for all of us – it is both.

If mankind survives another thousand years, historians of that era will remember a very distinctive thing about America that few of us think about these days. At the end of World War II the military our country was fully mobilized and had the resources to do something other nations had dreamed of but could never accomplish – conquer the entire world. My parents' generation, God bless them, declined to do so. (I have always felt that in the long view of history, America will be remembered for that among its other many accomplishments.) While recognizing an eventual threat to ourselves, earlier than necessary we sacrificed millions of our own people for the sake of others – and exacted no significant penalty or revenge upon the enemies we eventually vanquished.

America's military currently straddles the world – by necessity in some places and no longer necessary in others. Those efforts need to be reviewed in the light of current and future technologies that have altered how our military force can be used. When new capabilities afford us an opportunity to withdraw homeward, we should do so without delay.

America's economic might is also still the strongest in the world and will survive current challenges to its supremacy – but we do, as a nation, need to re-examine how we build on, distribute, and spend the wealth we've acquired over the last four centuries. Make no mistake about it – exploitation of our immense natural resources and the ingenuity of citizens permitted to act freely is the basis of our economic and cultural success. We need to be smarter about using the resources we have and be more humane in working with others to drive towards a brighter future for all Americans – and for other people across the world.

There is a morality in doing the right thing – even at the expense of the financial "bottom line" – that must be brought to the forefront in our dealings with everyone. Though many people may protest about the complexities of modern life, there is a simple rule that really never fails. When you put people first, everything falls into place – when you put money first, everything falls apart. America has experienced at least fifteen financial "panics", recessions, or depressions since the Constitution was established. [1792, 1796, 1819, 1837, 1857, 1873, 1884, 1893, 1896, 1901, 1907, 1929, 1973, 1987, 2008] Looking into the short stories of each validates that simple rule.

Moving forward through and beyond the 21st century, we should use that rule as a firm guideline to govern our behavior, both daily and long-term. Americans who put the weight of their own wallets ahead of the welfare of their fellow citizens should be recognized as selfish and unpatriotic, regardless of how much they proclaim love for the country they continue to disserve.

Companies and small businesses struggling to make ends meet to provide goods and services to their customers might gain sympathy about a reflex to conserve their assets during tough economic times. But large corporations, well-heeled financiers, and unprincipled speculators who twist and distort the workings of government and the market to maximize their wealth at the expense all Americans are worse than unpatriotic – they are criminals, moral criminals and sometimes even legal criminals. Americans must learn to lose their patience with these people who continually cheat them.

Let's repeat: **WHEN YOU PUT PEOPLE FIRST, EVERYTHING FALLS INTO PLACE – WHEN YOU PUT MONEY FIRST, EVERYTHING FALLS APART.**

When philanthropists have trouble falling asleep at night it's usually because they wonder how they can do more to help those in need. When people who love money have trouble falling asleep, their thoughts are turning around a different axis altogether. In the New Testament, St. Paul's actual quote on the subject is: "The love of money is a root of all kinds of evil". The descriptions above about improving our national perspective of money are not meant to encapsulate and cure all the evils known to the world. But they do show a way we can move towards a happier, more just society where all Americans – and all those who would like to become Americans – can rise to comfortable standards of living.

Issues sometimes brought up in modern politics like "family values", "prayer in schools", "right to life", "evolution's only a theory", and so forth ARE ALL RAISED WITH FALLACIOUS INTENT. The real issue, the only issue, is and always has been money – only money. Using those "values" terms in every recent election, the conservative power elite in America has crawled out from behind its executive desk and heavily recruited people in the evangelical church pews and double-wides across the country – recruited them to defeat their own best interests. Thoroughly washing their hands afterwards, they settled back into their leather chairs to resume worship of their own bank balances.

Either through a broad education program or a tightly focused "spotlighting" of individual issues, this cycle must be broken if America is to move forward forthrightly through the new century. At this writing I can think of no better course to recommend other than thoughtful discussion of the topics raised in this book.

The experiment of self-governance established by our current Constitution has been a model the rest of humanity tries to emulate. Their efforts are not always perfect – and sometimes get misdirected by dictators or would-be kings, but Americans can morally support the efforts of the world's citizens in their aspirations to become more like us. We, on the other hand, should not "rest on our laurels" but always look toward forming that "more perfect Union" the Constitution's Preamble dictates. For the coming century and beyond, some of the changes noted above should be contemplated.

For a number of years now, every President has finished nearly every speech or announcement with the phrase: "God Bless the United States of America". I'll posit something further: God blesses America every day – always has and always will.

Thanks very much for your attention. Now let's start talking about adopting some of these ideas.